Foundations
for
Reconstruction

Foundations
for
Reconstruction

by

ELTON TRUEBLOOD

> *If you have peace without justice, you will
> have neither peace nor justice.*
>
> —HAILE SELASSIE

HARPER & BROTHERS PUBLISHERS *New York and London*

FOUNDATIONS FOR RECONSTRUCTION

SECOND EDITION

B-V

Contents

Foundations
for
Reconstruction

Introduction

THE PROBLEM OF OUR TIME

In the great and moving drama of our age the prologue
has been completed. For a generation our ablest prophets
have told us that we were living at the end of an age and
now we know that this analysis was correct. We have
lived in "the end of our time" and we can date it. The
date was August 6, 1945.

The stage has been set, the chief actors have appeared
and the conditions of the coming struggle have been established. The prologue has been terrific, but a prologue
it has truly been. It has told us what the play is to be
about, but has given little hint of the outcome. Now we
know certain facts which thoughtful people everywhere
recognize. It is agreed that the maturity of technology
will be a dominant factor, that our world will be one
world for good or ill and that the fundamental systems
according to which human life will be organized will be
very few.

As the dramatic movement at the middle of the
twentieth century begins, we can be reasonably sure that

the long dominance of Europe is over, just as, five hundred years ago, the long dominance of the Mediterranean lands was over. For many generations Europe has been the chief center of organized life on this planet, with the rest of the world assigned to colonial status, economically, culturally or politically. This situation will not recur. The European countries may be remarkably restored and may even enjoy local spiritual revivals, but they can hardly recover their earlier position of world domination. It must be remembered that the decline of Europe is not tantamount to the decline of the West. The culture which we call Western, the fertile offspring of the union of Hellenism and Hebraism, may go on in other lands, even though Europe is in decay. But such continuity is by no means assured.

Our present century may be remembered by later generations as the century of successive threats to the dominant position of Western culture, threats both internal and external. There have been three specific and discrete ways in which the position of Western man has been challenged in our time. It has been challenged, first, by a conscious secession within the West itself. It has been challenged, second, by a direct attack from the outside, the first serious effort in modern times on the part of an Eastern nation to use the weapons of the West against the West. It has been challenged, third, by a distinct weakening of the central convictions and principles to which Western man has hitherto pledged allegiance.

The attempted secession from the culture of the West, which reached its climax in Nazi doctrine, has now been both defeated and discredited. It will not arise again in out time in this particular way, though it may be a threat in various clever disguises. Japan, following her crushing defeat, will necessarily become a minor factor for a long time, both materially and spiritually.

The first two threats to the position of Western man, the internal secession and the external attack, have already failed. In the form in which we have known them they are no longer live issues, though a slight change in events at the crucial point might have led to the success of either one. The remaining threat is the internal one of a slow disintegration. The two kinds of life which emerge from the preliminary struggles represent, in differing degree and manner, the breakup of the spiritual inheritance of the West. In Russia the break in continuity takes the form of overt and official atheism. In the victorious democracies it takes the form of an actual paganism combined with lip service to the ancient faith or, at any rate, an unwillingness to deny it. Which of these two threats is the more dangerous is hard to know, but it is at least clear that ours is the only one we can now do anything about.

We may truly say that the problem of the dominance of western man has centered about four different positions as follows:

1. Conscious secession—Germany
2. Quasi-secession—Russia
3. Outside attack—Japan
4. Quasi-loyalty—the Western democracies.

The other important logical possibility, that of conscious and convinced loyalty to the spiritual heritage of the West, has no representative in modern societies, though it is the one which, if seriously tried, might give the most reasonable hope for mankind.

As the preliminary struggle ends, we find that Western man has been able to reassert his strength. Some day the numerically greater part of mankind may be able to rise successfully against him, but that will be a long time from now. Western man is intrenched in his position of authority and power. He cannot soon be dislodged from the *outside*.

But he might be dislodged from the *inside*. The fact that the German secession came so near to success should destroy all easy optimism on that point for a long time. *What if it had been the ruthless Nazi minority who had first discovered a practicable way of producing the atomic bomb?* The difference this might have made in the history of mankind is beyond calculation. The point is that *other* forms of secession will undoubtedly appear and they may appear in those areas which now seem most safe.

The quasi-secession which Russia represents fills all thoughtful minds with questions. It represents such a variant on our tradition that it cannot truly be called Western any more, if ever it could. Perhaps we should coin a new term and call it "Northeastern." We could then say that the power of the earth is divided between those who profess a halfhearted devotion to the tradition of the West and those who demonstrate a burning devotion to the developing tradition of the Northeast.

There are now two great systems of life in relation

to which most of the movements of mankind in this century will necessarily find their places. The world has two poles spiritually as it has two poles geographically. One of these is a victorious, vigorous system which rejects, completely in theory, though incompletely in practice, most of the spiritual heritage of the Western world, particularly that of the Judeo-Christian tradition. It combines with this rejection a vigorous acceptance of science and the fruits of science, as well as a fierce idealism directed to the economic betterment of the common man, an idealism preached with earnestness, but without recognition of its ancient prophetic source. Russia is the only true representative of this system, though admirers in other lands, particularly in China, are numerous and no land seems to be without them.

The other primary system is our own. This system stands in the chief tradition of the West and is not conscious of any secession from it. In theory we combine the classic moral and religious heritage derived from Greece and Palestine with an economic system which seeks to provide the maximum individual liberty consistent with order and a thorough utilization of both science and the technical products of science. This system, like the Russian system, has emerged victorious from the preliminary struggles and with great consciousness of strength.

The dramatic movement, which has begun in earnest as the war has ended, will center largely about the relative dominance and mutual relations of these two systems. There is bound to be competition between the two gospels, each attracting adherents among those not now committed to either system. If this competition should get out of hand, and the will to peace should break down, the resultant clash could be tragic for the entire race. The resultant tragedy would far surpass in violence and terror anything that has occurred in the preliminary struggles. It would be the true Armageddon. This would constitute failure for all concerned and is the event which all men of good will must seek to avoid at all costs. For many the effort to avoid this must now become the major task in life. This task is dignified by the fact that the whole future of mankind seems to be at stake.

The relations between these two great surviving systems may take the form, not of competition, but of combination and accommodation. The political experience of Great Britain provides one local illustration of the manner in which such combination may be achieved. Great Britain now begins to combine the two modern systems in that she adopts a few of the features of the Russian economy, but without any philosophical conversion to dialectical materialism and with no conscious break with the moral tradition of the West. Other local combinations may be expected to arise.

As the dramatic movement proceeds there may be significant changes in the Russian system, possibly involving even a rediscovery of the revolutionary Christian heritage. In like manner there may be revolutionary changes in *our* system. Terrible as it may be to contemplate it, the truth is that our system might change by adopting, more and more, our own local brand of fascism, without once employing that ugly word. We might do this by such degrees that we should never be conscious, as the Germans so largely were, of an ideological alteration in our pattern. Many of our ties to our spiritual heritage are now so weak that we might break them without knowing that we had done so. If this should occur the world clash with attendant misery would be inevitable.

This is, in part, what makes the development of thought and action in the coming years so exciting. *We have no idea how it will come out.* We, like spectators at any great drama, are moved with both pity and terror, but we are more than spectators since we are actual participants in the action and may have some minor part in determining the outcome.

Most of us can have very little part in influencing the Russian experiment in living, but our own system is such that active individuals and groups can be truly effective at home. What is most clear, as we consider our own vocation in the struggle, is that the problem of moral reconstruction is the primary problem. No matter how powerful we are, and no matter how rich we are in physical resources, we shall decline as a people unless we can produce and maintain an ethical system that will make our great technological discoveries the boon to mankind which they might be, if rightly directed, and keep them from being the means of disaster which they may so easily be, and which, without such effort, they will certainly be. All this we have long known, but the release of atomic energy enforces the lesson so strongly that all people can appreciate it.

The logic of the situation which the atomic bomb symbolizes is as follows. *Though the atomic bomb is the fruit of science, the solution of the problem is not a matter of science, since it is admitted that there is no technological defense. The only hope, therefore, lies in world organization. Only world organization can insure that the fearsome invention is used by those forces concerned with justice and not by the lovers of irresponsible power. But since the world organization is dependent upon the trustworthiness of those concerned, the ultimate question is ethical rather than merely scientific or even political. The only answer to atomic power is moral power.*

The most sobering feature of the comparative moral situation is that the disciples of Marx and Lenin are sure of themselves and know what they believe, while so many of the upholders of the tradition of the West do not know what they believe or why they believe it. We have inherited a glorious ethical tradition which has inspired some of the best life this planet has known, but for millions of our people it is no longer a living tradition. We in the twentieth century have inherited a morality, but we have not thought deeply about it as we have thought deeply about scientific research. We put two billion dollars and a stupendous amount of intellectual labor into the Manhattan Project, but it does not occur to us that we should need to pay an equal price for success in an enterprise without which the Manhattan Project is catastrophic in ultimate effect.

Though we have inherited a morality, we seem to be incapable of reproducing it in living forms which we can pass on to our children. We prize our democracy but, for the most part, we pay no attention to the deeper convictions without which our vaunted democracy is practically meaningless and without which it could not have been produced in the first place.

The practical task of trying to restore the foundations of our democratic civilization is so immense that all who have any gifts which qualify them for this task should give their full energies to it. Every thoughtful person now knows that the major problem of our time is the ethical problem. Even the most superficial optimist now sees that we could destroy ourselves, and that the way we use power is far more important in the long run than is the amount of power we have available. The mandatory need of our time is the discovery or recovery of an ethical creed that can give Western man, at this juncture in his history, steady moral guidance.

Fortunately, we do not need to hunt for such an ethical creed. We already have it. We already have a cluster of convictions which belong to all strands in our culture. One of the ways in which our fundamental faith can be restored and reinterpreted for our time is by an attempt to state the moral principles which have provided, in large measure, the chief standard of conduct in the life of the West for almost two millennia. Many generations have given conscious assent to these principles, and other generations have accepted them as the unconscious basis of judgment in common life. Without these principles the whole history of the West would have been utterly different.

An important fact about these principles is that they constitute a cementing element in our cultural life. All three chief groups in our spiritual federation, Jews, Roman Catholics and Protestants, accept their validity.

This, therefore, is ground upon which we as a people can meet and from which we can move forward. Incidentally, this body of teaching provides material which *can* be taught and *ought* to be taught in our public schools. Many states forbid sectarian instruction, but this is not sectarian any more than the Twenty-third Psalm is sectarian. All children might learn:

> Above all else love God alone;
> Bow down to neither wood nor stone.
> God's name refuse to take in vain;
> The Sabbath rest with care maintain.
> Respect your parents all your days;
> Hold sacred human life always.
> Be loyal to your chosen mate;
> Steal nothing, neither small nor great.
> Report, with truth, your neighbor's deed;
> And rid your mind of selfish greed.

The Ten Commandments constitute the most memorable and succinct extant formulation of the ethical creed of the West. For that reason they provide a convenient statement of the fundamental basis of recovery and reconstruction. What is important, however, is not the particular formulation known as the Decalogue, but the total view of life of which the classic commandments are shorthand representations. Each of the commandments can be greatly expanded; each can be stated in positive rather than negative form and ought to be so stated. When this is done, what we have is not an outworn set of specific prohibitions, but positive principles of such a nature that a good society cannot be constructed or reconstructed without reference to them.

Though this book uses the commandments as convenient and suggestive chapter headings, it is not a book about the Ten Commandments. It is a book concerned with the philosophy of civilization. It seeks to discover the necessary planks for a platform on which civilization must be rebuilt if it is to be rebuilt in enduring fashion. That these planks correspond so nearly to the ancient formulations of the fundamental law is not surprising. We now know that the essentials of the classic formulation are by no means primitive, but represent rather the cumulative insight of the greatest of the prophets.

This small book is intended primarily as a manual. It is an effort to capture the ancient wisdom in the language of our day and situation. It is not maintained that all the developments suggested were envisaged by those who first prized these commandments, but it is maintained that this fundamental classification of our duties is permanently valid. We now know that the commandments, as they appear in the Biblical form, are the result of a long development, some of the stages of which are shown in other Biblical passages. What we have done in the spiritual life of the West is to continue this reasonable process, giving greater meaning and more precise application as we have faced the primary issues with disciplined insight.

The truth is that, in our task of rebuilding a shattered civilization, the ancient moral law comes to us again with startling relevance. It does not provide the superstructure, but it does provide the foundation, and it is the foundation which we must build first.

Chapter I

THE ALLOCATION OF PRIORITY

Thou shalt have none other gods before me.

The number *one* differs from all other numbers, not in degree but in kind. The step from two to three is relatively slight, but the step from one to two is enormous. A man who has two wives and a man who has three wives are in the same class; they are both polygamists; they are both able to divide their deepest affection. But both are totally different from the man who, because he cannot divide his affection, is wholly loyal to one wife. We preserve a fundamental insight in our grammar when we make the primary numerical distinction between singular and plural, no matter what the degree of the plurality may be. There is more essential difference between one and two than there is between two and a million.

In no realm is the uniqueness of singularity so significant as in our loyalties. Thus it is universally recognized that we cannot give complete allegiance to two nations;

we must *choose* between them. Complete allegiance to one eliminates the possibility of complete allegiance to another. In the same fashion men must choose, not only between states, but between the state and something else, so far as the highest spiritual priority is concerned. Since there can be only one ultimate priority the decision concerning what this may be is crucial for an individual or a society.

An illustration of the great practical importance of such ultimate choice among loyalties is provided by Martin Niemöller's remarkable book, *God Is My Führer.* This book explains why Niemöller went to concentration camp and why he refused the easy way out. He could not make any earthly creature his absolute master, because that would mean putting a mere man in God's place. *There can be only one Führer.* Pastor Niemöller's decision was clear; he could not worship *both* Hitler and God; therefore he chose God.[1]

The brave opposition to Hitler which was provided by Christian groups, as it was provided by no others in Germany, has amazed the world, eliciting the generous

[1] The radical decline of Martin Niemöller's popularity is one of the most curious phenomena of public opinion in our time. The American public first idolized the man and then largely turned against him, when it was discovered that he had actually volunteered for the German Navy. Apparently the public had gone on the false assumption that he was a conscientious objector, even against national defense. Actually he made a distinction between defending his country and giving idolatrous worship to Hitler. This is a distinction which we ought to be able to understand, inasmuch as many of our people would join the armed forces, while opposing the government. What we need to remember is that Pastor Niemöller was imprisoned for *eight years.* It is unbecoming of those who have lived in comfort to presume to belittle him.

praise of complete outsiders, such as Einstein. Many have been curious to know what the secret of this courageous opposition was. What did the church have that the labor unions and the newspapers and the universities did not have? We now know the answer. *They had the first commandment.*

Any people is safe from acquiescence in wanton tyranny if it keeps clearly before it the recognition that there can be only one ultimate loyalty and that the Living God is the only worthy object of such loyalty. This clears men's minds and makes them bold. Our historic religion leads not to an easy tolerance, in which all distinctions are blurred, but to the sharpest kind of distinctions. Pure religion is the final enemy of all totalitarianism because the worship of God will brook no rivalry. Few in our day have seen this as clearly as has Walter Lippmann in the following sentences:

They [the dictators] have seen truly that the religious experience must forever raise up new enemies of the totalitarian state. For in that experience the convictions which the dictators must crush are bred and continually renewed.[2]

Any state becomes dangerously totalitarian when it tries to take the place which is rightly God's place. The form which this action most commonly takes is the attempt of the state to become a teacher of faith. This is usually done by the formation of a nationalist youth movement which seeks to determine the spiritual life of the citizens. Whenever that occurs the state has overstepped its bounds and is potentially dangerous. The

[2] Walter Lippmann, *The Good Society*, Little, Brown & Company, 1937, p. 383.

state, in short, is evil whenever it tries to become a church as well as a state, thus eliminating the prophetic criticism of the independent church.

The state should be a policeman and a lawyer, but not a teacher of faith, for then it is claiming all of life and breaking the first commandment. Herein lies the profound significance of the principle of separation of church and state. The church and state must be separated, because this arrangement provides a beneficent check on the otherwise unbridled power of the state. Perhaps the greatest source of danger in the present situation of Russsia is that this beneficent source of internal criticism has been eliminated in practice. Since communism is a religion, though an inadequate one, church and state are essentially identical and the beneficent tension which separation of church and state provides does not exist.

Such considerations help us to see that the order of the Commandments is the correct order. Many have supposed that the order is out of date and meaningless for our time. The popular supposition is that the *ethical* commandments, such as those against murder and theft, are important, while the wholly *religious* commandments, the first four, are relics of ancient superstition. Many university professors have asked their students to reorganize the commandments in the right order of precedence, and the general experience is that more than 90 per cent of the students propose to *reverse* the Biblical order. It is doubtful if they realize that they are thus differing sharply from Christ, who was likewise asked to give the order of precedence. The first and greatest commandment, said Christ, is, "Thou shalt love the Lord thy God with all thy heart, and with all thy soul, and with all thy mind."[8] This, with its emphasis on the *total* allegiance required, is an ancient paraphrase of the classic form of the first commandment.

Quite apart from the judgment of Christ, however, the experience of brave men during the war should be sufficient to convince us of the rightness of the ancient order. It is important that men should not murder, and it is important that men should not steal, but it is far *more* important that they should have central convictions which give them courage to refuse to murder and steal, even when a tyrant may require it. This is why religion is always more primary, both in logic and in human experience, than ethics can ever be. To know what is right is important, but to have the power and courage to do it is far more important. We must never forget that Hitler was able to crush the mere moralists, but he was not able to crush thousands of men who thought the first commandment was *really* first.

The practical effect of such a conviction is to maintain a sense of the objectivity of truth and moral rightness. If God really is, and if He is the God of the whole world, there is one system of objective truth and our task is to discover it. Truth, then, is wholly independent of what may be temporarily fashionable or of what the present government may dictate. The Nordic myth cannot be made *true* by governmental pronouncement; it is still a lie if it was ever a lie. If the truth, then, is something to be discovered, something existing inde-

[8] Cf. Matthew 22:35-39.

pendent of us in the will of Almighty God, it can never be equated with something produced by a propaganda machine. "Nothing in the world is more dangerous or more false than a situation where a thing comes to be regarded as true or right if only a dictator or minister of propaganda says it often enough."[4]

The most dangerous of all philosophical ideas in our time is that of ethical subjectivism, according to which right is merely our own human creation and not part of the objective order. This is popularly expressed and supposedly upheld by the banal quotation, "There's nothing either good or bad, but thinking makes it so." Under rigorous philosophical analysis this popular or sophomoric view can be shown to be intellectually indefensible,[5] but the point we are making here is that such a view makes man helpless in the face of tyranny. If morality is merely a matter of subjective wishes or changing fashion, why is not one fashion as good as another? How could we condemn the man who kills his victims in a prison with a riding whip? Perhaps he liked it. Perhaps that is the new fad. But the thoroughgoing subjectivist has no logically valid basis of objection. He has taken a position which eliminates in advance all possibility of rational criticism.

The point to make is that, though the upholder of ethical subjectivity has no logical basis of opposition to tyranny, the believer in the Living God does have such a basis. If God is not only the author of nature but like-

[4] John Bennett, *Christianity—and Our World*, Hazen Book, 1936, p. 54.
[5] As in G. E. Moore, *Ethics*, Henry Holt and Company, 1912, Ch. III.

wise the God of history and the Source of the moral
law, we are dealing, when we deal with corruption,
with something as objective as is any physical substance.
Cruelty to an innocent child, then, is not evil because the
mores of our day say it is evil. It is evil because it is an
offense against the eternal moral law. It is evil because
this is God's world and every child, made in His image,
is infinitely precious.

The real believer in God, then, has a basis of action
which no nontheistic humanist can ever have. If there is
no ultimately valid criterion by which man's conduct
may be judged, who is to say *which* human tradition is
right? The tradition of wanton cruelty is certainly quite
as ancient as is the tradition of justice, mercy and truth.
Mere talk about the "rights of man" will not suffice. If
anyone wishes to uphold the doctrine of "white suprem-
acy," there is nothing in all the humanist armory of
thought to contradict him. The entire doctrine of the
rights of man is theological in origin and cannot be made
really intelligible apart from a theological basis.

The close connection between the doctrine of human
rights, especially the doctrine of human equality, and
ultimate theism is perfectly illustrated in the ancient account of Naboth's vineyard.[6] This is the story of a poor
man whose ancestral land was coveted by King Ahab.
In spite of the king's importunity, Naboth refused to sell
or to barter. Unwilling to be thwarted by Naboth's re-
fusal, Queen Jezebel took up the matter, arranged a false
accusation, with a farcical trial, and had Naboth stoned

[6] I Kings 21:1–20. The earlier story of David, Bathsheba, Uriah
and Nathan has the same point.

to death. Then King Ahab, supposing all barriers were removed, went to the vineyard to take possession, but he was mistaken in supposing that his acquiescence in his wife's deceit and cruelty had solved the problem. To his amazement and discomfiture, he found Elijah the prophet coming to meet him in the vineyard. "Hast thou found me, O mine enemy?" asked the king. And Elijah answered, *"I have found thee."*

Here is the fountainhead of the democracy we claim to prize. There *was* a limitation on the wanton power of the sovereign because there was *something* superior to the king. That something was the objective moral law which the government could neither make nor unmake. That something was the holy will of the Living God, which the prophet sought courageously to represent. The prophet, therefore, was the natural enemy of the would-be oppressor. As soon as this situation was recognized, a limit was set upon the dominion of men over men.

This story explains the fundamental basis of our democracy, because it shows the valid sense in which men are equal. Ahab and Naboth were not equal in wealth or power, but they were equal in that both were subject to the objective moral law. It is in this connection, and only in this connection, that a much disputed phrase in the Declaration of Independence makes sense. Those who criticize the statement of human equality, on the ground that men are not equal in intelligence or strength or ability, are merely uttering a truism that is far from profound. Of course men are not equal in most ways! In a merely humanistic context the statement in the Declaration of Independence is nonsense, since, apart from God, there is no human equality at all. But if God is, there is equality in a truly profound sense. Then men are equal in that all are equally accountable. The law is no respecter of persons, because God is no respecter of persons. He is the Father of both the humble and the proud. He is likewise the Father of both the evil and the good, for even at best our righteousness is filthy rags.

If we want to have *One World*, the only way to begin is by the recognition of our dependence on *One God*. All the other possible objects of ultimate loyalty are fictitious. The "Nordic God" does not exist and in the nature of things *could* not exist. God either is or is not, and, if He is, He has no rivals. It is ridiculous to talk about the "Japanese God" or the "white man's God" or the "American God." These are logical absurdities, and would not even appear in speech were our time not infected with the pervasive taint of subjectivism. What *we* happen to think about God is not very important; what God truly *is* is all-important.

Frequently we talk about the right of each man to worship *his* God. This indicates a major confusion of thought and a failure to rise to the level of true monotheism. What we should do is to speak of *God*, with no possessive pronoun at all. Equally offensive is the popular question, "Do you believe there is a God?" Why the indefinite article? Those who talk academically about *a* God are a million miles away from the brave men and women who not only believe in God, but worship him in humble trust with no reservations. They are not suffering and dying in loyalty to some abstraction; they have found Him who sustains them and leads them along the way.

If only men could gain in this tragic time a real sense of the love of the Living God, in the light of which all else is secondary, life might become radiant for millions. If God really is, that is the most exciting news in all the world. It means that we are not alone in our little efforts to maintain justice, mercy and truth and the freedom which they jointly make possible. It means that we may be supported and sustained. It means that there is a truth not of our making.

This genuine conviction would glorify life. Life is not glorified now because men do not really believe. This is almost as true of the churchman as of the professed heathen. A deep sense of the priority of the first commandment would change all men fortunate enough to share it. It would make us humble and it would make us brave. It is the first stone in the foundation upon which we must try to rebuild the shattered house which is man's home.

Chapter II

THE NECESSITY OF INTOLERANCE

*Thou shalt not make unto thee any graven image, . . .
thou shalt not bow down thyself unto them, nor serve them.*

The second of the commandments, in the classic formulation, is the one which seems to modern man the least
valuable of all. It seems to deal with idolatry, a practice
in which we have not been tempted to engage for more
than two thousand years. It therefore seems utterly out
of date and meaningless for our time. "How," the ordinary citizen of a modern nation may ask, "does an ancient and local stricture against the worship of graven
images have any bearing at all upon our time, and especially upon the reconstruction of our shattered civilization?"

Though the commandment which condemns obei-
sance to graven images seems to us the most trivial and
obsolete of all the items in the ancient code, it is an ar-
resting fact that the Biblical writers mentioned it more
than they mentioned any other commandment. Though,

in the Decalogue itself, the space allotted to the second commandment is surpassed by one other, the fourth, in the Bible as a whole the references to the second are far more numerous than are the references to any other. In short, the problem of bowing down to graven images was a live one to the people of Israel and their prophetic leaders to whom we owe so much of what is valuable in successive generations. If we are wise, we shall be slow to take lightly what was deeply important to so many whom we have reason to respect.

The prophets of Israel gave terrific emphasis to the second commandment because it referred to the greatest single danger of their people. *That danger was the danger of an easy tolerance.* The constant tendency of the people was to mingle with the local Canaanitish population and to adopt many of their ways. This tendency led continually to a compromise between the stern faith which the Israelites had brought from the desert and the lax or even obscene religion which was the practice of their neighbors. Their temptation was not the temptation to give up their faith in Yahweh, but rather the temptation to add to that faith in a tolerant manner, thus producing a syncretistic worship with various elements existing conjunctively.

The constant tendency of the people was in the direction of an easy and tolerant liberalism, while the great prophets were continual *protestants* against this tendency. The great prophets were uniformly conservative in that they resisted, through three crucial centuries, the temptation to indulge in the kind of toleration which blurs all distinctions. The prophets, therefore, were not *representative* of their times, but were *critical* of their times and thereby *productive* of new times. The characteristic prophet, from Elijah on, seemed a *narrow* man, resisting the desire to make an easy accommodation between things that are fundamentally different.

The prophets barely won! Time after time, new fashions arose which included Baal worship (a form of nature religion) or the worship of the bull as part of a fertility rite (the golden calf) or the astrological worship introduced from Assyria.[1] Why, the people asked, should they not be broad-minded and include these apparently harmless rites along with the worship of Yahweh who required of men that they should do justly, love mercifully and walk humbly? Why, they argued modishly, should they not say "both and" instead of "either or"? But one after another the prophets declared that the people must *choose*.

The prophetic way was a hard way, but it was the only way in which the noble tradition which we prize could have been preserved. We know very well what happened to those parts of the Israelitish population in which the syncretistic tendency won. It won because these people lacked the necessary prophetic protestations at the crucial time. The result was that they disappeared completely as a living tradition. This fate is really the fate which overtook the so-called "lost ten tribes." They were not "lost" in the sense that they migrated, to reappear eventually in other forms, as some have fantastically supposed; they were lost in that they ceased to be a people conscious of a unique vocation. Their descendants

[1] See II Kings 21:1-7.

became assimilated to other cultures and many of them live to this day where their ancient ancestors lived. The people of the southern kingdom escaped this fate, however, largely because, by Divine Providence, leaders like Ezekiel and "Isaiah of Babylon" were raised up during the period of captivity. The beneficent result of the "intolerance" of the prophets is that the most precious heritage in the world was preserved and is still our prized possession. Except for the insistence upon the now despised second commandment, this result could not have been accomplished.

The bearing of all this upon our present situation is as close and definite as could well be. We, of course, are in no danger of making a golden calf, in the literal sense, but we are in vast danger of following in our time the *same* easygoing pathway of which bull worship was once the local manifestation. In our day tolerance is almost universally regarded as a virtue and, by some, the supreme virtue. This is not wholly evil, since it may be better to be tolerant than cruel, but it involves so much of evil for our total civilization that we are forced to challenge the popular sentiment if we seek to rebuild our society in an enduring fashion.

The present high regard for tolerance is shown by many clichés which pass for conversation. "Each man has a right to his own view," is one. "A man's religion is his own private business," is another. These seem, superficially, to have a certain validity, but they will not stand up under analysis. Does each man have a right to his own view if, for example, his view involves violence to his fellow men? Is the religion of the fanatical Jew-hater his own business? Obviously it is not, since his religion may affect greatly the welfare and happiness of other men. Is the religion of Father Coughlin his own business?

Freedom of religion has been widely announced and upheld as one of the Four Freedoms, but it is doubtful if most of us have analyzed what it means or have understood what it is we are supposed to be upholding. When we begin to probe beneath the surface we find that what great numbers of our people mean by freedom of religion is merely a glorified indifference. They think, and some of them say, that they believe in freedom of religion because they believe religion to be *unimportant*. Belief in freedom, then, is a high-sounding name for what is actually contempt. Great numbers of our people, who are themselves wholly pagan in their lives, pride themselves on being wonderfully tolerant in matters of worship. Their real meaning is something as follows: "I can't understand, for the life of me, why anybody wants to do anything so silly as to worship God, who probably does not exist, or to spend a Sunday morning in a stuffy old church when he might be horseback riding or swimming at the beach, but I certainly won't do a thing to stop him. I tell you I'm broad-minded in these matters! I don't care whether a man is a Jew or Christian or whatever; I won't stop him; and if I want to be a pagan I don't want him to stop me."

This is the lowest intellectual level on which the contemporary glorification of tolerance appears. It cannot, of course, stand up at all under rigorous analysis. The point is that God either is or is not. If God is, that is tremendous news and the reasonable man will make the effort to understand God's will correctly the most serious business of his life, to which all other pursuits are ancillary. If God is not, it is high time we found it out and began to eliminate all the nonsense. The awful truth is that *if belief in God is not a true belief, it is evil.* If God is not, then all the effort that goes into public and private worship is a waste of human energy and ought to be brought to a speedy end. The upshot is that a serious thinker can have great intellectual respect for a convinced atheist, who works at the job of attacking theism. He is in any case following the logic of his position to its consistent end. But the serious thinker cannot have any intellectual respect for the merely tolerant man, because the tolerant man is essentially stupid.

The sober truth is that we cannot make a decent civilization by following the modern fashion. It will take stronger stuff than this to build among the ruins of a world so near to catastrophe. What the world needs, far more than it needs a fashionable tolerance, which is fundamentally patronizing in spirit, is a burning faith which can change men's lives. Great advances come in culture, not when all distinctions are blurred in a hazy and jovial good will, but when sharp distinctions are made, distinctions dictated by the truth. Power comes not by supposing that one view is as good as another, but by finding, in honest inquiry, what the objective truth seems to be, and then following it with stubborn courage tempered by humility. *There can be no cutting edge that is not narrow.*

The new spirit we need in our distraught time will not come by some vague thing called "religion." To talk about religion is often a convenient way of avoiding talk about God. Above all the new life will not come by discussion of "spiritual values,"[2] which may mean anything, including a spirit of good fellowship toward others of the white-collar class. One of the most searching of contemporary European thinkers, himself secretary of the World Council of Churches, has aroused many by the following pointed query: "Why does modern man use the word 'God' as little as possible and the word 'religion' as much as possible?"[3] The author gives a partial answer to his own question by saying, "Behind this enthusiasm for religion and this shyness about God there lies a shifting of our outlook on life. To put it briefly, there has arisen a profound uncertainty among us about the ultimate and objective realities of life, and a corresponding tendency to cling to the less elusive realities of subjective human experience."

This is it precisely. When men fail to believe in God in a straightforward and objective sense, they stress their own subjective experiences. Then, in place of having faith in God, they have faith in "science" or in "religion." But both science and religion are human pursuits. Therefore when we make them the objects of our veneration we are guilty of idolatry, for idolatry is the worship of the products of the human mind in place of the worship of the Living God.

[2] Much of the discussion which has marked the new enthusiasm for the "humanities" in our universities is on this level. Frequently the "values" mentioned are treated as purely subjective. Wherever this is the case the contemporary enthusiasm for studies in the humanities is not a hopeful sign, but a sign of decay.

[3] W. A. Visser 't Hooft, *None Other Gods*, Harper & Brothers, 1938, p. 28.

This insidious tendency has gone all through our present societies. There are courses in "religion" in our colleges in which any strong affirmation of faith in the God of Abraham, Isaac and Jacob would be considered bad taste.[4] In all circles we find many who, even when they do use the word "God," admit, under questioning, that what they really mean is a subjective feeling in them, not something as objective as men and houses. Some do not even realize that, by this process, they have departed wholly from the heritage to which we owe more than to any other.

The modern interest in "religion" may not mean anything at all, so far as the restoration of a vigorous and just civilization is concerned. Religion is of various kinds. It may be unutterably lofty, as in the words of Isaiah 53, or it may be wholly debasing. The priests of Baal were "religious"; the organizers of temple prostitution are "religious"; the Nordic Christians are "religious"; but all three are a million miles away from the worship of the God and Father of our Lord Jesus Christ.

The great question, now as always, is not whether we shall be "religious," but *which* religion we shall prize and foster. There have always been more false religions than true ones, as there are now. The now discredited Nazism is an example of a religion, full of power, which was almost wholly evil. Communism, as upheld by many of

---

[4] Sometimes these are courses in religion taught from a supposedly disinterested point of view. Our very nomenclature is revealing. H. G. Wood has pointed out that many are willing to have departments of religion, but few are willing to inaugurate departments of theology (the science of God). See his inaugural address upon his appointment to the professorship of theology at the University of Birmingham.

the Russian youth, is also a religion, but instead of being wholly bad it has some good elements in it. Because it has not included the cult of irrationalism, as Nazism did, it may even have within it the seeds of its own reformation.[5] Those who believe in reason might eventually become really reasonable and worship the *Author* of all reason.

Meanwhile there is a faith which includes, at the same time, the respect for reason which produces science and the respect for the sacredness of personality which produces true charity. It is the hope of a regenerated world now as it has been before. It, if taken seriously, can do for our time what it did for the decaying culture of classical Greece and Rome. But it will never do this so long as we go on saying that one faith is as good as another or that a man's religion is his own private business. It cannot do it, unless our faith again becomes a burning faith, eschewing the fashionable and patronizing tolerance of our generation. This burning faith will substitute the spirit of the true missionary for the spirit of easy tolerance. The entire situation is altered if we leave behind our adolescent discussions about religion and speak instead of *God*, whom we have neither invented nor created, but whom we have come to know as the Lord of Life in the tragic days of suffering and of promise in which we have been assigned to live.

[5] Cf. Jacques Maritain, *The Twilight of Civilization*, Sheed & Ward, Inc., 1943.

Chapter III

THE RECOVERY OF URGENCY

~~~~~~

Thou shalt not take the name of the Lord thy God in vain.

The kind of tolerance which obscures the necessity of choice between competing faiths is an evil thing, but there is another mood which is almost equally dangerous for our society. This is the mood of those millions who claim adherence to faith in the Living God, but who would be ashamed to get excited about it. That would be bad form. The faith is harmed far more by such timid upholders than it is by open and violent enemies. *The worst blasphemy is not profanity, but lip service.*

It is instructive to note that there is not, in the entire Decalogue, any explicit condemnation of intellectual atheism. The commandments are all addressed to *believers.* Jesus stood in this tradition when he directed his strongest censure, not against the avowed pagans or infidels of his day, but against those who claimed to be believers. He made it plain that to say "Lord, Lord" has no value at all, if those who use the words do not take seriously what he said.

The first commandment is in condemnation not of those who fail to believe in God, but of those who get their ultimate priority wrongly placed. The second commandment is not against atheism, but against the fashionable tendency to suppose that one way is as good as another. The third commandment does not condemn those who fail to believe; it condemns *those who believe and do nothing about it.*

There are at least two good reasons why sheer atheism is not condemned. In the first place it is rare, and was even more rare in ancient times. Possibly it was nonexistent. In the second place it is never really dangerous. It is a dull and unexciting position to hold. Atheism, once it is fully understood, makes men sad. To come to the conviction that there is no spiritual power supporting and sustaining puny men is bound to make men very sad providing they are intelligent.[1] Since it is obvious that there is not much hope if man really stands alone, only a superlatively honest man would adopt such a view. But superlatively honest men are seldom dangerous.

What is dangerous is not intellectual atheism, which is unpopular, but mild religion, which is very popular indeed. What is dangerous is not a frank rejection of the Judeo-Christian faith, which has been the chief inspiration of Western civilization for almost two thousand years, but the acceptance of that faith in an *attenuated and meaningless form.* And this is to take God's name in vain. It is to give lip service to moral standards, but

[1] Cf. W. P. Montague, *Belief Unbound*, Yale University Press, 1930. "Atheism leads not to badness but only to an incurable sadness and loneliness." (P. 67.)

not to take them seriously. The sin lies, not in rejecting God's name, but in taking His name, *without a sense of conviction and urgency*.

There is little doubt that this is the ordinary situation in the West today. Certainly it is the position in America, which we know best. We resent it terribly if some critic says we are not a Christian nation. We have churches, don't we? Don't we have prayer at the opening of Congress? But it takes no very great sophistication to know that these are superficial evidences of the faith. That they *are* superficial is becoming increasingly evident, and the best evidence of this is that we do not expect the faith to make a radical difference in our entire mode of life. It is both cheap and easy. In short, it is empty.

We may therefore say truly that the one ancient commandment which is most completely pertinent to our contemporary predicament is the third. Of all the commandments it hits us hardest. It hits us hardest because it reveals our life at its weakest point and shows us that we cannot be saved except by a return to veracity and urgency. As though we could not bear to face its challenge directly, we have developed a clever technique for avoiding the criticism implicit in this command. We have told ourselves that it is concerned with profanity, but profanity, as everyone knows, is recognized by all as a mere peccadillo. By making the commandments refer to minor sins, we are in a most comfortable position, since either we do not commit these minor sins or, if we do, it is obvious to all that they have no great importance.

But the third commandment does not refer to profanity, as we normally understand that word. It refers to something far more fundamental in our lives, something that is conspicuous in thousands who would be ashamed to utter vulgar oaths. And even the uttering of oaths is evil only in so far as it illustrates, in one small way, this deeper sin which the third commandment exposes and condemns. To take God's name in vain means to "take up for unreality." It is to express a faith but without enthusiasm. This deeper meaning becomes clearer as we note that the parallel in an older code reads, "And none shall appear before me empty."[2] *An empty, meaningless faith, a faith not taken seriously, may thus be actually worse than none.*

There are four fundamental positions that we can take in the contemporary world in regard to faith in God Almighty as revealed in Jesus Christ. One alternative is an open rejection of the faith in favor of some pagan system, usually a system based on a mystical doctrine of race. This alternative was taken in different forms by both the official Nazis and by those who sought to employ Shinto as a support of Japanese expansion. In the Nazi teaching, at least, the issue was clear-cut and definite. There was a conscious and deliberate rejection of the Judeo-Christian glorification of humble service. The notion that the highest type of manhood is demonstrated in humility and love was contemptuously rejected in favor of a scheme which glorified the fierce beauty of the beast of prey. The best philosophical support of this alternative faith is found in one strain of the teaching of

[2] Exodus 34:20. The essential order here is the same as in Exodus 20 and Deuteronomy 5.

Nietzsche, and the most moving artistic expression is found in some of the music of Wagner.

This alternative to the Judeo-Christian faith is now widely supposed to be nonexistent as a result of the overwhelming defeat of the Axis powers. But we may be assured that this optimism is premature. The open glorification of Nordic brutality as against the "Jewish myth" is of course in disrepute, but we may be sure that it will arise in coming years in various disguises, some of them clever and some of them stupid. We must, accordingly, be on our guard and we must understand that this avowed paganism will probably arise in new and hitherto unexpected places. We may still be occupying Germany while it arises at another point, perhaps in one of the victor nations. We shall then be locking the old barn while the new barn is robbed.

The most likely form that such paganism might be expected to take would be that of a new religion. The new religion might be a modern version of some ancient heresy such as nature worship or the deification of blood and soil. Such religion might be expected to arise in a tired and fed-up culture. Its great opportunity would consist in the fact that most of our people are spiritually empty and therefore uncritical. Having never heard of Christianity as a dynamic faith, they might become easy marks for some fancy new faith presented with vigor by a demagogue. That this has happened in one part of the West during our lifetime should at least destroy our complacency.

The second alternative is the official position in Russia.

This combines a rejection of Christianity, intellectually, with the strong acceptance of some practices which stem from the gospel, especially a vigorous brotherhood which transcends differences of race. This system has a great appeal in many parts of the world, chiefly because of its humanitarian idealism, but it still includes much that is very cruel. Furthermore, there is little hope for its true success in providing an ideal social order, so long as it resists the kind of internal criticism which a living and free church provides. There is very little evidence that the reinstated church organization of Russia is either living or free. What evidence is there, for example, that the Soviet government would permit vigorous criticisms, such as the last two Archbishops of Canterbury have leveled at the British government?

The Russian alternative likewise involves serious intellectual difficulties, especially those connected with the official espousal of a particularly dogmatic philosophy, viz., dialectical materialism. The official doctrine of the universal pervasiveness of the class struggle is one which can be shown to lead to contradictions. The official Marxist philosophy holds, on the one hand, that the class struggle is a natural reality, like the laws of nature, yet, on the other hand, it urges men forward to a situation in which the class struggle is ended by the rise of the classless society. After quoting Lenin to the effect that there is a parallel between the natural and the social sciences, in that physics teaches the existence of positive and negative electricity, while social science teaches the class struggle, one of the keenest critics of Marxism has put the matter as follows:

If the class struggle is parallel to the tensions of nature, then it is something healthy, normal, constant, and cannot be ended without disaster. Moreover, if it is strictly natural and necessary, all moral criteria are irrelevant. The textbook says, "Planets presuppose the sun; capitalists, the proletariat." But if the relation of capitalists to the proletariat is analogous to the relation of the planets to the sun, what on earth is wrong with it? It is part of the natural order and the one relation may endure as long as the other.[3]

Though much of contemporary Soviet ideology may thus be shown to be intellectually uncritical and its mood both dogmatic and doctrinaire, it is bound to be looked upon by millions as a live alternative. We may describe it accurately as the extreme example of our cut-flower civilization. *It is trying to keep the fruits and flowers of our Christian faith, especially its benevolence to the common man, not merely in neglect of the Christian roots, but in open denial of them.* In this the Russian system differs from the democracies, which constitute a cut-flower civilization in that they *neglect* what they do not have the courage openly to *deny*.

The third alternative, then, is our own, and is seen characteristically in Anglo-Saxon lands. We disdain the open paganism of the Nazis; we fear the frank and atheistical materialism of the Communists. Our solution lies not in the acceptance of the gospel as the very breath of life for a people in great danger, but in maintaining the respectability of a supposedly Christian ideology wholly devoid of the mood of urgency. Many of our real con-

[3] H. G. Wood, *Christianity and Civilization*, The Macmillan Company, 1943, p. 55.

victions can be shown to be as pagan as those of the Nazis and as materialistic as those of the Communists, but we seldom admit it. We pride ourselves on being an essentially devout people (though not in the churchly sense, of course), and we prove it by allowing the ancient maxim, "In God We Trust," to remain on our coins.

This alternative which we have worked out, and which may be termed the American Way, is exceedingly clever of us. It avoids so many difficulties. It avoids association with all that rather nasty stuff propounded by Hitler, for example, but it avoids at the same time all the hardships and difficulties which would be involved if we were to take the gospel seriously. We make the best of both worlds. We are equally shocked at hearing the faith rejected and at seeing it practiced. In short, we have learned, in our cleverness, how to take God's name, but take it *in vain*.

Many of our pulpits are occupied these days with outcries against paganism and infidelity. These things are assuredly evil, but they are not the real enemy which we face at home. The real enemy is not irreligion but *vague religiosity*. The real enemy is not the Red organizer who openly opposes the church but the respectable citizen who adopts a patronizing attitude toward the church by the gesture of joining it, when he has no idea of genuine commitment to its gospel. The person who needs most to be convinced is not the open sinner but the man to whom has never occurred the idea that true religion is always revolutionary in both individuals and societies and is consequently exciting.

Ours is the third way and it will not really succeed, even though it now seems to be partially successful. Our true condition is hidden from us, partly because of our phenomenal wealth in resources and partly because we are profiting by inheritance from a generation which took the faith with far greater seriousness than our own. Our ancestors believed a gospel which involved the note of urgency because it was concerned with damnation and salvation. It had a masculine vigor about it. Ours has become "Christianity and water" with both the urgency and the vigor gone. In any case the problems of the world are so great that they cannot be solved by those whose convictions are halfhearted. The crisis is too deep for that.

Not only will our mild religiosity fail to support a sagging civilization; it cannot long maintain even itself. This is not a condition in which men can long remain, especially when they are living under strain and conflict. Such a culture exists in unstable equilibrium. The ancient classic world tried to remain on this level, but found that it could not really do so. As the crisis advances we shall leave this temporarily pleasant middle ground and we shall either become openly pagan or we shall be driven to the fourth alternative, that of commitment to the will of the Living God in a radical Christianity that is not ashamed to be frankly missionary and evangelical. The fourth alternative is the creation, throughout our culture, of the Fellowship of the Unashamed. Ours would then become one of those glorious ages of revival, but we are a long way from that now.

Chapter IV

FREEDOM FROM THE ANGELIC FALLACY

Remember the sabbath day to keep it holy.

The most common form which the mild religion of our day takes is that of individual religion, with little or no reference to the church or to public worship or to any established religious observances at set times. This is almost universally supposed, by those who practice it, to represent an advance on churchgoing. The characteristic modern is not *ashamed* of his failure to support and attend church or synagogue; on the contrary, he is proud of his relative detachment. He supposes that he has gone on higher. He may be tolerant of his few neighbors who still support and cherish what seems to him an outgrown institution, but he certainly is not tempted to follow their quaint example.

Such a man, who is undoubtedly the characteristic man of our century in the West, is often personally kind and may actually demonstrate several of the Christian virtues. If he ever thinks about the matter at all, he supposes that he has graduated from churchly or ecclesiastical religion, with its demand for worship at least one day a week, and has adopted in its place what he may call "spiritual religion." This spiritual religion is independent of organization, of places or times of worship, and of all creeds. "I get closer to God on the golf course," says the solid citizen, "than I ever do in the church."

This supposed emancipation from forms and ceremonies can sound very noble as well as advanced and modern. The position gets most of its plausibility from the fact that bears a superficial resemblance to a great teaching of the gospel, the teaching that God can be known and loved in *any* situation. The spiritual giant has no need of external supports. But the vulgar truth is that most of the people who pass off the wretched cliché about their devotion being to Christianity rather than "churchianity" are not spiritual giants! Men might conceivably have great experiences of God's presence, and their own moral need, while getting out of the rough by the seventeenth hole, for nothing is impossible with God, but such an experience is not really *likely* to occur.

One result of the modern notion that individual religion is better than institutional religion is the contemporary estimate of the fourth commandment. Most people seriously believe that the commandment concerning the Sabbath is both trivial and anachronistic. It is, they think, almost as meaningless for our day as is the second commandment, which concerns graven images. It seems to our neighbors to be the perfect example of a command which may have been applicable once, but is now outmoded, in our enlightened day, because it is *purely cere-monial*. It is something outgrown because it is narrowly religious rather than ethical.

Let us try now to examine this modern assumption with all the logical rigor we can summon. The first fact we note is that, whatever we may think of the command about the Sabbath, it holds a place of vast importance in the Bible; it is not considered a trivial detail *there*. It is, indeed, the longest of the laws in the Decalogue. It holds a great place, not merely in the formulation of the law, which we might expect, but in the works of the proph-ets, which is another matter.

The reason for the great emphasis on the Sabbath in ancient Judah was that this institution was one of the major instruments of cultural survival. When Jerusalem fell, in 586 b.c., and the leaders, their temple having been wantonly destroyed, were taken to Babylon in captivity, their chance of survival was slight. The northern king-dom had fallen more than a hundred years earlier and had never been revived. It has not been revived to this day. The southern kingdom would have gone the same way, and the whole of Western civilization would have been greatly impoverished thereby, if the prophet Eze-kiel and others like him had not placed great emphasis on the Sabbath. The Sabbath observance became an ex-ternal badge which held the people together as by a public witness. Once each week the people stood up to be counted in their alien environment and, though the weaklings naturally fell away, the faithful were conse-quently strengthened.

Along with this emphasis on the Sabbath, which had

such a beneficent effect in the life of the refugees, came the invention of the synagogue. Having no temple, and being far from familiar or sacred scenes, the great prophets of the Exile produced real novelty. In the sixth century before Christ there arose the practice according to which people came together to listen to the reading of the moral law and thus not only to worship God but to be strengthened in their personal lives. Thus arose both the Sabbath and the meetinghouse, which are taken for granted in Western civilization but are known in no other civilization, except by derivation or direct borrowing. We are more in debt than we usually realize.

The point is that the institution of Sabbath congregational worship saved a precious heritage from extinction. If the refugees in Mesopotamia had had nothing but private and individual religion, such as is so fashionable now, they would not have survived as a people and we in the Western world would never have had the Bible or the great teachings that have, along with those derived from Greece, been formative in our culture. Mere individual religion does fairly well in prosperity, but something stronger is needed in a genuine crisis.

The more we think about the matter, the more we see that the popular view is wrong and that our civilization cannot be rebuilt unless institutional religion is revived and loyally supported. The chief reason for this is that human nature is weak. We have high purposes, but we fail dismally to live up to them. Consequently we need all the external supports we can find, to add to our feeble strength. Here the dictum of the great Dr. Johnson is priceless in that it states the point so perfectly that no one has been able to improve upon it. "Every man," wrote Johnson, "naturally persuades himself that he can keep his resolutions, nor is he convinced of his imbecility but by length of time and frequency of experiment."[1]

It is the common human experience to need to be reminded of what we know to be true. To provide the needed reminders is one of the chief functions of the glorious rhythm of the week, which the Sabbath makes possible, and the services of public worship, which the institution of the Sabbath facilitates. We may be convinced that humble service is better than strutting power, but our dedication to the right way is greatly enhanced if we hear again the great words of the Bible or join in singing with our fellows the classic hymns which have supported the resolves of frail persons like ourselves for hundreds of years. Perhaps I have known it already, but I am wonderfully helped by hearing once again, "The Lord is nigh unto them that are of a broken heart; and saveth such as be of a contrite spirit."[2] Though I might have heard it a thousand times, I could always be made a better man by sharing devoutly in the Collect for the Fourth Sunday after the Epiphany:

O God, who knowest us to be set in the midst of so many and great dangers, that by reason of the frailty of our nature we cannot always stand upright; Grant to us such strength and protection as may support us in all dangers, and carry us through all temptations; through Jesus Christ our Lord. Amen.

---

[1] Samuel Johnson, *Prayers and Meditations*, Meditation for June 1, 1770.
[2] Psalms 34:18.

Even with the help of such magnificent reminders and supports, we are bad enough. What might we be without them? Even those who have separated themselves wholly from public worship, and yet show evidence of good lives, as many do, obviously owe part of their character to the effect of these external supports in their youth. A great many of the men in public life, who now feel superior to the church, had the first fifteen or twenty years of their lives greatly influenced by the external helps to character which only the church provides. What such men seldom consider is what either the world in general or their own personal lives would be like if the external supports, which they now despise, had never been. Would any of them really prefer a society in which the rhythm of the week, which the Sabbath makes possible, were unknown and nonexistent? Do they really advocate a kind of life in which the many sponge on the few?

That this is actually the situation may be shown by a single crucial case, that of marriage. If the upholder of a churchless religion were consistent, he would arrange for his daughter's wedding in an office of a justice of the peace, since that is the alternative to the kind of marriage which the church and the church alone makes possible. That is the logic of secularism. If each man were to follow his own practice, there would be no sacramental marriage service, no place to celebrate it and no one to perform it. But the man who is so proud of his emancipation from church is not consistent. He seeks to arrange for the greatest events in his family life so as to take advantage of a surpassingly beautiful thing which he has not earned and which, if his example were followed, would not exist. It is, therefore, easy to demonstrate that this modern man, who sounds so lofty in his spirituality, is really a thief and a parasite.

Part of the difficulty with the man who is a parasite on the Christian community is that he has never asked himself the right question—what the world would be like if his own practice should become standard practice. He misses the point by supposing that the question is: "Do I personally want to attend worship on the day of rest?" But this is a silly question. No decent culture can be built if that is the sort of question that is asked. The real, the pertinent question is this: *"What is required of me as a responsible citizen of this place? What is my duty in keeping alive the continuity of culture which has helped to save this world from being a worse madhouse than it is?"*

The fundamental mistake which is made by the man who holds that he is religious while he disdains the offices of the church is an error of the mind rather than an error of the heart. He is committing what we may call *the angelic fallacy*. He makes the mistake of supposing that he and his fellows are angels when, in reality, they are men. If we *were* angels it is doubtless true that we should not need the external supports which institutional religion gives. We might not need to be reminded of our duty, we might not have the fierce temptations of the flesh and the fiercer temptations of the mind. We might then worship as well by the seaside, among the hot-dog stands, as at the altar. But *we* do not happen to be made that way.

The wisest of men have known all along that we are men and not angels. Even the saints report lapses. The great philosophers have always known that man is a feeble reed, even though there is hope in him. Thus a distinguished philosopher of our own day expresses the convictions of other disciplined minds when he writes:

I am impressed by the weakness of men and their dependence on help; I see my own humiliating limitations. . . . To fall on our knees and supplicate for pardon and help seems to me not an abdication of our manhood, but an acknowledgment of our sin, an act of wisdom and of an enlightened will.[3]

The angelic fallacy is really part of the romantic belief in natural goodness, which is now so discredited on both moral and intellectual grounds. The noble savage is not noble! He is merely savage. It is only by virtue of great care that life can be made decent. There is no human decency or justice that is not *contrived*. The fundamental reason why men need the ministrations of the church is that human life, left to itself, has a natural bias toward evil, a bias which is abundantly demonstrated by the fact that our most ideally constructed communities are tainted with the struggle for prestige and personal power. The way out lies not in despising the help which the Bible, the church and the Sabbath can give, but in using them as reasonable incentives. Man is such a creature that he dare not neglect what Dr. Johnson called "the incitements to do well." Much of the reason for the relative success of the Christian religion in dealing with

[3] Paul Elmer More, *Pages from an Oxford Diary*, Princeton University Press, 1937, p. xxv.

raw human life arises from the fact that it has long pos-
sessed a truly sophisticated psychology.

We have now tried for most of a generation the experiment of churchless religion. That this is our present
condition is evident from the fact that vigorous church
members are strictly a minority in our present culture.
But we have not done so well. The Western democracies
have come safely through the ordeal of war, thanks
partly to natural resources and partly to a fortunate
alliance with Russia, but this does not mean that our
civilization is safe or that it is really a success. On the
contrary, we are now experiencing what can only be
described as a moral slump. This is indicated by many
phenomena, among them the alarming increase in both
divorce and murder.

The error of anticlericalism, as W. H. Auden has suggested, lies not in what it says about the clergy (which
may be justified), but in its *implied flattery* of the laity
(which is unjustified). The clergy may be valid objects
of censure, but this does not mean that the laity are virtuous. In fact they are not! In the same way the error of
the upholder of individual religion lies not in the censure
he levels at our poor little churches, for that censure is
wholly justified. They are as bad as their critics say and
worse. Only the loyal insider knows how truly bad they
are. The error of the devotee of individual religion lies
not, therefore, in his criticism of those inside the
churches, which is correct, but in his implied flattery of
those outside the churches, which is erroneous. The awful truth is that the sinners are quite as bad as the saints,
and sometimes worse. The man who goes horseback rid-

ing on Sunday morning, instead of attending church, may be quite as self-centered as the man kneeling at the communion rail, but with this enormous difference, *that he is unaware of it and consequently doing little or nothing about it.*

One of our worst mistakes in strategy, especially in Protestant circles, has been to minimize church attendance. We have said, endlessly, that real religion is an affair of the heart and that no particular rite or ceremony is *necessary*. In this we have told the truth, but it was a half-truth, and, like all half-truths, profoundly dangerous. No external ceremonies are *necessary*, but many are *extremely helpful*. People have understood us to say that attendance at public worship was of slight or trivial importance, but that is a genuine falsehood. Attendance is of vast importance. And the sooner we begin to say this the better.

The purpose, of course, is to encourage the religion of reality which goes far beyond forms. External helps are important, not for their own sake, but precisely because they are helpful in leading frail and forgetful humans into what may truly become a religion of reality. To make the means into ends is a grievous mistake, but it is not the mistake of this generation. The equally grievous mistake of this generation is to fail to achieve the end because we have neglected the means.

The primary problem is not that of keeping the Sabbath or even of encouraging divine worship. The primary problem is that of trying to make a decent life for mankind on this planet at this tragic hour. The reason for supporting the churches, feeble as they are, is the realistic one that we are not likely to have a decent life on this planet without the contribution which they alone can give. The sober fact is that the Christian churches and the Hebrew synagogues are the only organizations in our civilization whose *primary* purpose is to keep alive the moral and spiritual principles without which a decent world is impossible.

Chapter V

RESPECT FOR INHERITANCE

~~~~~~~~

Honour thy father and thy mother, that thy days may be long upon the land which the Lord thy God giveth thee.

There are many, in our contemporary society, who are willing to accept the argument up to this point as cogent, once it is presented to them. They can see that there is little chance of rebuilding on enduring foundations unless the lost urgency of our religion is recovered. They can see, moreover, that this requisite urgency cannot be cultivated and maintained by men working alone, apart from institutional religion. Many would agree with Professor Baillie when he says: "I cannot be a Christian all by myself. I cannot retire into my own shell or into my own corner and live the Christian life there. A single individual cannot be a Christian in his singleness."[1]

A recognition of this truth makes many see that a saving faith must be institutionalized, accepting boldly all

[1] John Baillie, *Invitation to Pilgrimage*, Charles Scribner's Sons, 1942, p. 119.

the dangers that institutionalism involves, if it is to live and be effective in our social order. Many will therefore agree, when the case is thus presented, that there must be a church or something like it in our society and that they, consequently, ought to support the church, not only by attendance and by financial sacrifice, but also by the application of their best thought to the regeneration and revival of the church as a living organism.

Though many thoughtful people will go this far, it is precisely here that they stop. They do not go on to give loyal support to their *own* church, the only one they are really in a position to assist and influence. Instead of working with the poor, feeble, actual institution in which they have been nourished, and which therefore has a valid claim upon them, thousands in our day dream of an ideal church. Judged by this ideal, the actual denominational church, of which they may be members or which might provide a natural vehicle for them, seems so wretchedly inadequate that they give it up as hopeless and refuse to work with it at all.

Here is the familiar human situation in which perfectionism is really a hindrance to progress. *The abstract best actually becomes the enemy of the concrete good.* Loyalty to the *Church* may be self-defeating because it hinders many men from what is most important in practice, loyalty to the *churches*. Much of the devotion to the ideal church of our dreams is fundamentally an escape mechanism, which eases our consciences for our failure to work actively for the betterment of the local church to which we belong or ought to belong.

Much of our talk about the Church is delusory because the Church, apart from the individual churches, is an abstraction. If they do not exist, *it* does not exist. You cannot be a member of *the Church* unless you are sharing actively in the life of *a church*. The missionary movement, as a whole, is a grand and glorious thing, providing some of the brightest examples of courage which the crisis has elicited, but there would be no missionary movement apart from the thousands of feeble little churches, such as the one around the corner, Ladies' Aid and all.

The excuse which the "emancipated" frequently give for failure to work in the actual churches of their communities is their revulsion against denominationalism. They say that they cannot abide the bickering between the sects and that they are unwilling to give aid or comfort to any particular sect. Denominationalism, they like to say, has almost destroyed the power of the Christian religion by dividing its forces when they ought to be united.

There are several important and pertinent replies which the honest analyst must make to this monotonously repeated complaint. The first is that such a criticism is uninformed and woefully out of date. Usually the person who makes such a remark is betraying the fact that he is still judging the world, at least religiously, by the supposed conditions of his childhood, uncorrected by later experience. There may have been a time, long ago, when the Methodists fought the Presbyterians and the Presbyterians fought the Baptists, but this is certainly not the present situation. On the contrary, we are living in a time when there is a wonderful spirit of co-operation among the denominations and a great sense of sharing in a common enterprise. The ecumenical movement is one of the gigantic advances of our generation and *it has not come from pharisaical critics on the outside; it has come from devoted and self-critical men and women inside the denominational groups.*

This new sense of a common task, which makes most of the talk about sectarianism so deplorably out of date, is evident in any great contemporary gathering of Christian leaders. In a noble gathering, such as the annual Pastors' Convention of Ohio, attended by at least two thousand four hundred registered delegates, it is literally impossible to tell, by anything they say, who is an Episcopalian, who a Quaker and who a Congregationalist. They all have essentially the same message, in the face of the world crisis, and they listen to speakers with practically no regard to the speaker's sectarian affiliation. In the same way, the men invited as guest speakers at our university chapels practically never raise any sectarian issues. As one university president said, "I can't tell which is which, because they all say the same thing." The upshot of this is that a modern critic who complains about excessive sectarianism is hitting a straw man. The churches have many present evils, but this one is largely a thing of the past.

A second pertinent answer to give to the person who excuses himself from work in the local church on the ground that it is sectarian is that any living church is *bound* to be sectarian. *There is no vital religion in the world today that is not sectarian and there cannot be.* The reason for this is rooted deeply in human nature.

We naturally form into groups and find our best life in reasonably small fellowships. Like-minded fellowships in different committees strengthen one another in conscious loyalty to a heritage. Such groups are called denominations. There is nothing very dangerous or surprising about this and certainly there is nothing about it that is unique to religion. We do it in everything else, as the existence of lodges, political parties and service clubs so abundantly testifies. It is very curious, indeed, that a man who takes for granted the existence of separate organizations for Rotary, Kiwanis and Lions Clubs should profess to be shocked by the fact that Christians are organized in a similar way.

The inevitability of such denominational organization is demonstrated vividly by the so-called community churches, priding themselves on being nonsectarian. They have hardly come into existence, when they begin to organize quarterly and yearly conferences of the various community churches. But this simply means that they have become new denominations. It is the universal fate of those groups which have arisen in opposition to denominational Christianity, with avowed loyalty to a wholly nonsectarian faith, to add one more to the list of denominations. Nor do those who call themselves Catholics, whether Anglican, Roman or Greek, avoid the promotion of denominational mentality by the magic of a word. They are denominational in spirit, cultivating a unique kind of fellowship in each case.

It is time we ceased wasting our breath lamenting the existence of sects and began to realize that the separation into denominations is often as *beneficent* as it is *inevi-*

table. Those who are loyal merely to "the whole of truth," disdaining to bother with the small bit they can handle, are likely to end by helping not at all. The world is too big to deal with all at once. Truth is advanced by a sensible division of labor, each group emphasizing one aspect which might otherwise be forgotten, but with complete respect for other groups.

Another important consideration is that denominational loyalty frequently opens the way to the kind of friendship which men and women most need. In countless towns the best way in which new people can make friends is by beginning to attend a church with which they have had some denominational affiliation in another town or state. Many of the smaller denominations provide a genuine freemasonry in which a great many of the members know each other in spite of geographical barriers. Anyone who despises this does not understand much about the needs of common men.

Perhaps the most beneficent effect of sectarian ties arises from the way in which denominational religion may help people to glory in their own heritage. In short, it helps them to honor their fathers and mothers. Personally, I have always been greatly strengthened by the fact that my people on both sides have been Quakers for more than two centuries. This has never tempted me to despise non-Quakers or to suppose that other heritages are less honorable, and it has not hindered my loyalty to the Church Universal any more than my loyalty to my state has hindered my loyalty to my nation. What helps me is participation in a tradition and a noble tradition. Since I did not choose it, I am not free to let it down. I have a heavy responsibility to see to it that the torch shall not fall from my hands, before I pass it on to those who come after me.

All who care about our culture, and are consequently worried by the moral slump which is demonstrated in so many particular ways, must agree that we dare not allow the most important single means of moral development to go unemployed. Now there is very little difference of opinion, among those who have thought deeply about the moral education of children, concerning what the most powerful influences are. It is widely agreed that character is formed, not primarily by overt moral teaching, but far more by the sense of belonging. People grow by virtue of social membership, because they strive to live up to that of which they are supposedly a part. Conscious membership is the most powerful single stimulus in all human behavior. The mere notion of sharing in the life of a particular family may be a great incentive to better living. There are many who remember all their lives the special standards of their families, so that they can say, when a crisis arises, "Browns don't do that."

Now the point is that denominational loyalty is precisely the sort of thing we need in the formation of character. Secular society can provide nothing equal to it. For many of us who were fortunate enough to have our childhood at the beginning of the century, before the start of our Thirty Years' War, there were local churches that were decisive in their pervasive influence. It may have been a modest church in the country, but, wherever it was, we loved it. I can remember best the scenes outside the meetinghouse door, when the meeting was over and the neighbors were having their visit of the week. My father lies buried there now, but then he was one of the neighbors. I remember, with especial gratitude, one man who always treated me as an equal, by discussing with me the changes of weather and the prospects for crops.

Charles Morgan speaks for many of his age when he writes, with powerful tenderness, of the village church of his boyhood:

. . . Left to oneself, one might have chosen the garden, not the sermon, and yet, when the decision was made and the little procession had set out, the power of ritual asserted itself—not yet the ritual of the Church, but that of the fields, the bells, the angle of the sun, of other figures approaching down the convergent lanes of the hill opposite. In the churchyard, if the five-minute bell had not yet begun, there was a pause for neighbourly conversation, and it was possible to wander among the graves and read again an inscription which, long ago, had been learned by heart. Inside the church itself was a mingling of daylight and lamplight, a pallor of glass which would presently darken, a low gleam of stone and wood; and all these things bespoke the hour and the month, and were part of the order of the seasons.[2]

There are many, slightly younger than we are, who, unfortunately, never had such experiences. Some of them were victims of the awful heresy that children are fit only for Sunday School and are not able to profit by participation in grown-up people's services, with the attendant sense of belonging. Some were the victims of

[2] "The Village Church," *The Times Literary Supplement*, June 3, 1944, p. 267.

the general secularization of our whole society. Many are the children of parents who have despised their own heritage, supposing it to be narrow and cramping, and have ended, not by giving their children a more inclusive heritage, but by disinheriting them entirely, so far as our major tradition is concerned. The parents, being a bit ashamed of the narrow-minded churches of their own youth, have ended by giving their children *none*.

There are, thus, two levels on which nonsectarianism appears in our time, but the levels are so far apart that they have almost nothing in common. One level is that of the positive ecumenical spirit, which believes so heartily in the underlying unity of the entire Christian movement that it will spend any amount of effort in trying to make that unity effective. It was positive and aggressive nonsectarianism such as this which was responsible for the planning and execution of the great ecumenical conferences before the war, chiefly those held at Oxford, at Edinburgh and at Madras. The late Archbishop of Canterbury, William Temple, was an outstanding example to the whole world, of this level of experience. He was so truly catholic in spirit that he was driven by the purpose to pull men together in a positive fellowship which transcended ordinary boundaries.

One of the chief marks of this higher nonsectarianism is intense loyalty to the particular tradition in which the devout man may be placed. Archbishop Temple, in his surpassing loyalty to the ecumenical movement, was not the less loyal to the Anglican tradition, where the greater part of his tremendous energy was spent. The larger loyalty, in such a man, does not exclude the smaller one, but the smaller one becomes one of the most effective ways, when rightly understood, of promoting the larger.

In great contrast to this is the lower and now modish level of nonsectarianism. While the higher nonsectarianism becomes a means of *inclusion*, the lower becomes a means of *exclusion*. The fact that the churches are not fully united is used as a reason for not working in *any* of the now divided churches. The ultimate effect of this is wholly negative, since we shall never have the Church as it *ought to be* without working with the churches as they *are*.

Discouraging as it may seem, it is only by placing individual stones that we can build a wall. Our civilization desperately needs the firm wall which only a truly united Church can provide, but we cannot build it except by building individual churches. And the normal place for the average man to begin is with the church of his fathers.

Chapter VI

THE CULTIVATION OF THE UNEASY CONSCIENCE

~~~~~~~

Thou shalt do no murder.

Our cumulative argument concerning the reconstruction of our society has now reached the point at which we are ready to consider the specific ethical convictions without which a decent society cannot endure. If we are clear about the right allocation of our ultimate loyalty, if we make the distinctions which lead to a sense of urgency, and if we are careful to employ rightly the external institutions that support our feeble individual efforts, we are well on the way, but our platform is not complete. We need to find objective points of reference in our moral order. We must find the plumb line by which our human constructions are ultimately to be judged. Unless we do, we are bound to build what Virginia Woolf so appropriately calls "The Leaning Tower." What we seek is the true vertical as judged by reference to the eternal stars.

The ultimate moral principles of a people are revealed,

not by what they *do*, but by the way in which they de-
fend their actions. When we try to tell *why* an action
is right, we necessarily do so by appealing to more ultimate and profound positions which we assume our op-
ponents will accept as fully as we do. Thus it is highly
instructive that the use of the atomic bomb, which killed
so many innocent people in two Japanese cities, was almost universally upheld, by virtue of the fact that it
saved human life. Its use was defensible, President Tru-
man and many others argued, because, however horrible
its immediate effect may have been, it saved millions of
lives by forcing a speedy end to the fighting. The un-
argued principle here, the one which supposedly requires
no argument, is the principle of the sacredness of human
life.

That this principle is truly a valid one almost all persons in our present society agree. This is the most easily
accepted of all the planks in the classic moral platform.
We all suppose we understand it and that it is so clear as
to demand no elaboration. Any discussion of it might
easily appear to be a waste of effort, inasmuch as nobody
doubts it; there is no one who upholds wanton killing.

Simple as the moral law against murder may seem, it
is easy to show that it is really a very perplexing one,
involving us in many difficulties when we concern ourselves with its actual application to concrete human situations. Certainly it is not possible to avoid moral difficulties by the simple expedient of never taking life, as
some theosophists try to do. This is no solution, because
we are faced frequently with a choice of *which* life is
to be taken. Will you kill the lice which carry the typhus

germs or will you let the typhus germs kill the people? On the highest grounds, a person who *can* kill the lice, and refuses to do so, is terribly evil. He seems to be avoiding the issue, but his very avoidance is really taking sides. He is valuing lice rather than men. For this reason the sensitized conscience realizes that lower forms of life must frequently be sacrificed for the sake of higher forms of life.

The Biblical statement of this aspect of the moral law represents true sophistication in that it is not "killing" that is condemned, but "murder." And since murder is nothing other than "unjustified killing," it is clear that the principle involved is something more subtle than the mere determination never to take life. The words of Christ bring a further refinement into the moral situation by the insistence that the real sin lies deeper than the mere act of murder; it lies, says Christ, in the hatred of the man who seeks to murder. Thus the man who tries to murder his neighbor, but is hindered by circumstances beyond his control, is quite as evil, from a strictly moral point of view, as the man who is not thus hindered.

If it were to stand alone, the moral law against taking human life would be almost meaningless. Life, we may grant, is better than mere dirt, yet why get so excited about it? Certainly it is silly to get excited about the destruction of a louse. But is it not also silly to get excited about the destruction of a slightly larger creature who may also carry germs at times? If a man is a mere organism and nothing more, all the talk about the sacredness of life is rather stupid. If a man is just a highly complicated mechanism, soon to wear out, there is not any cogent reason for valuing him so highly. When one machine wears out we turn to another. There are many machines and there are many men.

Though talk about the sacredness of life is stupid, on the ground of naturalistic assumptions, there are grounds upon which it makes sense. If God really is, if He is the Author of all created things, including living things, and if man is made in God's image, as no other creature is, the pattern of thought begins to change. The individual man may be a dull or sinful creature, but if he is truly made in God's image so that, with all his sin, he is capable of eternal fellowship with God, and if, moreover, he is one for whom Christ died, then at last we begin to see why we should value human life.

Physically man isn't very great, and mentally he is replaceable. No man is indispensable. Morally we are all of us far from good, and even our righteousness is filthy rags. Our highest flights of human planning are spoiled by the self-centeredness which we can never wholly escape. *The only conceivable basis on which our common human objection to murder can be logically defended is therefore the theological basis.*

If man is merely a sample of a racial bloodstream, as Hitler taught, it is wholly reasonable to kill men as easily as Hitler killed them. Hitler was consistent. It is *we* who are inconsistent. We are trying to maintain a moral position without reference to the only logical basis which can support it.

That mere life is not what is precious is shown by the fact that almost any sensitive or courageous man will gladly give up his own life for a cause. If it is mere life that must be preserved at all costs, this is always a ridiculous action. But there are many reasons for which a brave man will willingly die and there are many situations in which it is agreed that it is unworthy for a man to continue to live. It is one of the beneficent effects of the Christian gospel that there is a sense in which we have been taught to think lightly of life, at least of our own lives. "He that would save his life, loses it," has sunk deeply into our consciousness in the West. The most moving single fact about Christ, the fact symbolized by the Cross, is the fact that he valued his physical life with a lightness that has seemed to men divine.

Sometimes our great concern over the continuance of physical life is an evidence, not that modern man has a high respect for man, but rather that he has a low one. Often the sheer materialist is more eager to keep life going than is the genuine believer in God. This is wholly understandable, since the materialist has no hope beyond the grave, whereas the Christian is convinced that this life is but the tiny beginning of an endless existence. It is noteworthy that sheer pagans often put more emphasis on the preservation of the body after death, by means of expensive vaults, than Christians do. A consistent Christian will put *no* emphasis on the body after death, for he believes that "this mortal must put on immortality."

The conclusion to which we are driven is not that it is life which is sacred, but that it is personality that is sacred. The sixth commandment, which appears to be concerned with the negative principle of the condemnation of murder, makes sense only when it is transmuted into the positive principle of the necessity of genuine valuation of persons.

Individuality is the true locus of value. We do not *value* the materials on which we experiment in the laboratory; we *use* them. When one is spoiled we throw it away and take up another, and this is the only ground on which experimentation is possible. All real experimentation with human life is revolting, and this is one of the chief reasons we have had for being thoroughly shocked at the Nazi human laboratories. By the same token, if it had been *true*, as some have asserted, that our use of the atomic bomb in Japan was undertaken in the mood of experiment, then we must conclude that the act was horribly evil.

What is so terrible about war is not that men die, for they will die eventually anyway, but that war encourages men to think of other human beings, not as sacred individuals for whom Christ died, each precious in his own way, but as *experimental targets*. The evil of war is the philosophical evil that it makes us think of our enemies, not as *persons*, but as *things*. The bombardier aims, not at *persons*, but at the *target*. We hypostatize the enemy into a single resistance and speak of *him;* but the enemy is not a *he;* the enemy is *they* and the they includes individual human souls from tiny babies to old men and women, women like my mother.

The only practical solution of the problem of the sacredness of life is the cultivation of the uneasy conscience. Animals must die to feed humans or to save them from disease. We must deliberately give them infantile paralysis if we are to save boys and girls from this dread malady. *But* we must never do this wantonly or easily or gladly. It is one of the great merits of the moral philosophy of Dr. Schweitzer that he has emphasized this point in such a way as to catch the attention of contemporary thinkers everywhere. This is probably the most valuable of all the contributions which this gifted man has made. The essence of Dr. Schweitzer's contribution is expressed in the following paragraph:

Those who test operations or drugs on animals, or who inoculate them with diseases so that they may be able to help human beings by means of the results thus obtained, ought never to rest satisfied with the general idea that their dreadful doings are performed in pursuit of a worthy aim. It is their duty to ponder in every separate case whether it is really and truly necessary thus so sacrifice an animal for humanity.[1]

If it is important to cultivate an uneasy conscience concerning the death or suffering of animals, it is a thousand times more important to cultivate such a conscience in regard to the death or suffering of human beings. It is admitted that some human beings must sometimes die to save other human beings or to save a way of living which will dignify and beautify other lives, some of them as yet unborn. All this we are forced to accept if we are reasonable and not merely sentimental, *but we dare not let ourselves get used to it and therefore take it lightly*.

Our hope lies in keeping that kind of sensitivity which

[1] Albert Schweitzer, *Civilization and Ethics*, A. & C. Black, 1923, p. 262.

never allows us to accept death or suffering supinely. War may come again and, if it does come, brave men will sacrifice themselves rather than permit the sacrifice of others, but to glory in this situation would be the ultimate blasphemy. We ought to be bitterly ashamed of any human society which limits young men to these alternatives.

The Christian church has often held that there are conditions under which it is right for a Christian to participate in war, because the alternative may be worse than the fighting, but it is to the credit of the church that it has always maintained, following the great example of St. Augustine, that the Christian must face war with sorrow and misgiving. Some Christians share in war and some do not, but all Christians know that war is *tragic*.

During the past few years something terrible has happened to our minds in that we have become hardened to human pain and death. Once we were terribly moved if ten or twelve were killed in the wreck of an airplane. Now we can read in our evening paper that millions of the little ones of our former enemies are at the point of actual starvation and we put the paper down and go to the table, erasing the awful fact completely from our minds.

This is an evil thing that has happened to civilians quite as much as to those in the armed services. We cannot build a healthy society so long as it exists. We need a recovery of sensitivity if we are to rebuild our broken world. We need to remember that the death of a child of God is one part of the world is quite as tragic as is the death of a child of God in any other part. We must recover the capacity to be shocked.

But this, like any good thing, will not come of itself. It must be contrived; it must be cultivated. This is the task of our spiritual leaders. Men must be made tender again. The cultivation of the uneasy conscience is a major plank in the platform of reconstruction. We have started the task of reconstruction if we begin to convince men that *the good conscience is an invention of the Devil.*

Chapter VII

THE ACHIEVEMENT OF FIDELITY

Thou shalt not commit adultery.

There are many in our present society who when they talk about morality mean sexual morality. A person who is arraigned on what our newspaper jargon terms a "morals charge" is someone accused of an offense involving the relations between the sexes. Sometimes there are people who even suppose that the chief function of religion is to legislate for men and women in this particular area of human experience.

All this is, of course, grotesquely false. Morality is not a matter of one particular set of human acts, but of all human actions. Moral questions are questions concerning a decent life in its entirety and the relationships between the sexes constitute only a fraction of the totality which we seek to make as good as we can. We begin to realize how false the popular use of language in this regard is, when we note that a person may be wholly innocent of any sexual offense and yet be a thoroughly evil person.

Those who have never committed adultery may be detestable in character, especially in the free employment of personal slander and talebearing.

Though popular speech is thus wrong in making sexual offenses equivalent to immorality, there is a partial justification for the ordinary language in the fact that sexual corruption is one of the chief symptoms of a sick and decaying society. The right ordering of the relations between the sexes is so important to a culture that any culture which fails to deal realistically with the problem is likely to go to pieces. Gross sexual indulgence, such as marked the life of ancient Rome in its later periods, is both the symptom of general decay and the cause of further decay. The most obvious form that a rotten civilization takes is an absurd emphasis on sexual pleasure both in practice and in literature.

Observing as we can the experience of Rome in the days of its apparent power, but real decay, we realize that our own system of life is in jeopardy. If our civilization ever loses respect for marital fideldity, giving itself up to an orgy of indulgence, our society will fall with a terrible crash, no matter how externally powerful and rich we may be. We have not yet reached such evil days, but there are many evidences that we are going in that direction. Unless we can *change* our course, nothing will save us.

In any realistic approach to the problem we must recognize how very powerful and how nearly universal the sexual urge is in the human race. The desire to mate comes early and is strong long before marriage is a practicable course to follow. If we are honest we admit that, in a great many of us, this desire occupies a considerable share of conscious thought and that it continues, in one way or another, throughout a normal lifetime.

That it occupies a very large share of our literature is obvious. If we should take out of our literature all that refers to love-making, both respectable and illicit, how much would be left? The amount of humor or alleged humor which has the mating urge as its ultimate basis is enormous. All this is clearly recognized in the Bible with no mincing of words. Young people who try to sneak out of libraries the bold books which deal directly with amorous situations could get what they seek without any trouble by looking in the Bible. Confession stories, which many suppose are very bold, can hardly be more straightforward than is the Bible when it tells the story of David and Bathsheba. How straightforward the Bible language is may be seen in the following from Deuteronomy: "If a man be found lying with a woman married to an husband, then they shall both of them die, the man that lay with the woman, and the woman: so shalt thou put away evil from Israel."

The main lines along which the mating urge should be handled are fortunately clear. Sex cannot be wholly repressed and no sensible person would want to repress it if he could. Sexual life can be a thing of very great beauty, an inspiration to countless men and women. This beauty comes neither by repression nor by unlimited expression, but by *discipline*. Apart from discipline the sex urge can become an ugly and a harmful thing, destroying both souls and bodies of the persons concerned.

There is very little danger now of repression, since

that has no advocates, but there is enormous danger of the opposite mistake, the glorification of license. This glorification of license is part of what parades as a "philosophy of life" to the effect that men and women should obey their urges and do whatever is "natural." This comforting philosophy seems to some to derive sanction from what they call "modern psychology" though they would find great difficulty in securing any actual verbal support from any reputable psychologists. The popular view, however, seems to be that "psychology" advises men to let nature take its course so as to avoid unhealthy complexes.

This notion of doing whatever is "natural" is one of the ideas that will not bear up under critical analysis. What if all men were to follow their nature? It might be one man's natural inclination to seduce the wife of a wounded soldier lying helpless in a hospital. Should he therefore do it? It was natural for Hitler and his accomplices to torture innocent men in Dachau and other camps. It is natural for many to murder. But we need go no further. No man, except a lunatic, would uphold these "natural" acts.

The word "natural" when used in a moral context means almost nothing. It is natural for man to kill. It is also natural for man to discipline his mind and heart so that he refrains from killing. Since these are equally natural, the word is so ambiguous as to be meaningless in this important context. A life wholly uninhibited and undisciplined would be a wholly disorderly life and furthermore it would be a short one. Complete repression, as we have said, is out of the question, but a person who has not learned to say "no" to his urges has not begun to understand the nature of human life as contrasted with mere animal existence. We must sometimes say "yes" to our urges and we must sometimes say "no," but we must say "no" far more often.

In avoiding the erroneous extremes we must be careful, as Jesus taught, to reject the position of the censorious critic, devoid of human tenderness. It would seem from the Gospel story that Christ was more tender toward sexual offenders than toward others. Note his shaming of the men who accused the woman taken in adultery with his memorable utterance, "Let him that is without sin cast the first stone."

Actually the sexual sin may be a minor sin, a sin of mere bodily temptation, and one which easily merits forgiveness. This is especially true of the sin of the person in the transaction who has been the victim of another. But should we be equally tender toward the seducer? Would Jesus have been so uncritical if the person caught had been the man who was the woman's partner?

The real sin in fornication or adultery is not the act itself, which is purely biological, but the degrading effect on human character. Prostitution is wrong because it degrades the prostitute, making her a mere tool for the satisfaction of man's desire rather than a human being respected in her own right. The philosophical basis for the judgment that sexual license is morally evil is really the Kantian formulation of the categorical imperative, "So act that thou dost treat every human being as an end and never as a means merely." But this is a roundabout way of formulating the Golden Rule of Jesus, "Love thy neighbor as thyself." You aren't loving your neighbor as yourself if you merely use her.

Some things that men do are harmless, trivial pastimes *and they are a man's own private business*, but sexual relations never belong to this class. They always affect another; they trifle with human affections and loyalties; they harm or help others; and they may involve the bringing into the world of new human beings. This is the realistic reason why all talk about free love is basically silly. Free love would make sense if it were like playing solitaire, but it isn't.

This is why the sixth and seventh commandments have always been closely associated, so closely, indeed, that they appear sometimes in the order we are following and sometimes in the reverse order. In the Greek Old Testament, known as the Septuagint, the law against adultery precedes the law against murder. Both rest on the same foundation—the sacredness of human personality. It is wrong to tamper with affections and it is wrong to tamper with human life, and both acts are wrong for the same reason.

So great is the temptation to sexual indulgence in socially harmful ways that we need something powerful to control us. Where shall we find it? The answer lies in a noble conception of marriage, especially marriage seen as genuinely sacramental. Marriage, as slowly developed in our Christian culture, is one of the glorious products of our faith. What it means is that one man and one woman determine to unite their two separate destinies. They stand before an altar, dedicated to the worship of Almighty God and, engaging together in a religious act, they freely pledge, in the presence of their friends, their lifelong devotion.

The power of this sacrament in human life is incalculable. It takes great emotion and glorifies it by directing it in a single channel. The life of two together can be far more wonderful than can the life of two lived separately, especially when there are children who really belong to *both*. Instead of denying sexual experience, Christian marriage accepts it and glorifies it.

It may seem a gratuitous paradox, but the truth is that marriage is more important than love. Marriage is more important than love because it is the normal situation out of which true and abiding love arises. The popular notion, much encouraged by light fiction and the motion picture, is that love is primary, marriage being a dull anticlimax. But this is vast error.

Real love hardly exists outside marriage. How could it? Real love is a slow growth coming from unity of life and purpose. *Love is a product.* It is a thing to be created by mutual service and sacrifice. Normally this service and sacrifice can exist only between married people and only if the bond is accepted as a permanent one.

Love outside of marriage or *before* marriage is largely a romantic fiction. Before marriage there is a certain amount of passion and the mutual attraction which is the *possibility* of love. This is a good starting point, but it would be a very weak conclusion. The Hollywood mentality is in error because it supposes that this weak thing is love and that it is of primary worth.

In the Western world we have greatly overemphasized romantic courtship. That the vigorous love produced by marriage can be achieved without this romantic prelude is proved by the undoubted success of arranged marriages. The success comes not because the couple have been "in love," but because sacramental marriage is so powerful in human lives.

All who have any sophistication are aware that the choice of a mate is usually an accident of geography. Any one of several persons might, under auspicious circumstances, have been chosen as a life partner and with equal success. Marriages, then, are not made in heaven, but *marriage* is. For marriage is the way in which the most beautiful things men know are produced. It is the way in which a terrific urge is made into a blessing instead of a potential curse.

How is fidelity, which is so important to our civilization, to be achieved? There is only one practical way and that is the sense of reverence which marriage as a sacrament encourages. Certainly the problem cannot be solved by medicine, important as medicine is. Much has been made in recent years of the prophylactics which make men safe from venereal disease. But they do not even *touch* the main problem. All that they can do is to enable men to fornicate with relative safety. They do not bear on the question of fidelity and the construction of a sound society of mutual faith.

In this great field the practical approach is the religious approach. We have inherited, in our religion, an institution of amazing beauty, but it will not maintain itself. The modern tendency is to destroy it. Note the rising popularity of serial polygamy. Note the tendency to take marriage lightly as a temporary convenience. The great and good thing we have made can be maintained only by constant vigilance and care. That is why the seventh plank in our moral platform exists.

Divorce is coming to be more and more common, so common indeed that any sound philosophy of civilization must include reference to it. That divorce is sometimes justified we cannot doubt, because there are situations in which the marriage really no longer exists. When all the reality is gone, when there is no longer mutual trust and unity of destiny, marriage is largely a fiction. All this we now recognize and ought to recognize. But in recognizing it we are in great danger of falling into another and more serious error than that of strictness, the error of looseness. If divorce should become so easy and so normal that it is looked upon as a live possibility, even at the moment of marriage, our society is already broken down.

Divorce, though sometimes justified, must always be looked upon as *failure*. A divorced couple must see that they have failed in the most important undertaking of their lives. Divorce may sometimes be the lesser of two evils, but in any case it is evil and we dare never look upon it with complacency. In short, if our society is to be strong and the lives of children protected, the marriage vow must be taken with complete seriousness. It must become a matter of conviction. It is interesting to note that there is some progress in the Bible in regard to divorce, but that the movement is not, as we might suppose, toward greater looseness; it is a movement toward greater strictness.

We often wonder what we can do to help, when we

see the enormous danger to our civilization. We see it falling in some places and we want to hold it firm. Sometimes we feel keenly our inability to do anything. But here is something which almost every common man and woman can do. We can hold our life firm at the crucial point which concerns the foundation of the family. Every person who resists the temptations to mere indulgence and tries to keep marriage sacred in his own experience is rebuilding the world. It is in such ways that a culture is made. A culture rests partly on material resources, but it rests far more on fidelity, and fidelity is something to be *achieved*.

Chapter VIII

THE DIGNITY OF OWNERSHIP

Thou shalt not steal.

Sometimes we are tempted to say that money is unimportant. The major thing, we say, is the life of the mind or the life of the spirit, in both of which we are above the claims of the mundane world. Actually, most such talk is nonsense. Money is vastly important, especially when one does not have it. Any superiority to the temptations connected with property is chiefly possible only to those who are personally well endowed by inheritance and therefore free to do what they please. But a haughty contempt for "things" is not very impressive when it is combined with a secure income derived from tax-exempt securities, managed by a trust company. The "unselfishness" of the man who never stoops to accept remuneration for his labor is hardly convincing if the man is fortunate enough to have no need of earning.

There is a sense in which men and women must live above material considerations, as St. Francis partly did in the thirteenth century, and as Gandhi partly does now, but the proposition that the higher life is independent of possessions is simply untrue. Sometimes the ownership of great possessions is a real barrier to the promotion of the life of the spirit, but far more often the lack of possessions is an almost insurmountable barrier. The chief reason why money is important is that the lack of it leads not only to personal hardship but to terrible rivalry and to lasting bitterness. It is perhaps logically *possible* to be a high-minded person when living in a situation as crowded as is the Negro section of any city, but it is highly improbable that it should be done.

Anyone who ever heard the late G. A. Studdert-Kennedy talk about money can never forget the experience. This modern prophet said that the real meaning of money was brought home to him when he saw a girl dying of tuberculosis while she lived "in one of those abominable pigsties which do duty for houses for a considerable portion of our population." The girl *could* get well, but only on one condition: somebody had to find enough money to transport her to a decent place where she could have fresh air, professional care and good food. Studdert-Kennedy went out and got the money and then he knew, he said, what money is. "It is the power to demand a human service and to be sure that you will get it."

It is because money and property can mean so much in human welfare, in the means of knowledge and in the opportunity to appreciate beauty that we ought to value it very highly. We ought to value it, not for itself, but for what it will do in our own lives and in the lives of those for whom we care. "If any man says to me that he does not love money," writes Studdert-Kennedy, "I immediately begin to wonder whether he is a madman, a millionaire, or a tramp, those being the only types of people I can imagine saying it with anything like sincerity."[1]

It is only when we begin to understand, in some fullness, the human significance of money that we see why stealing is wrong and why no decent society is possible unless its wrongness is recognized. It is wrong to steal a man's property because you may, by doing so, take away his opportunity of providing for his family the education, the health, the food and the privacy which they, as beings made in God's image, deserve and require. A society in which a man might labor for the sake of his loved ones and then have his competence taken from him by those who happened to be stronger, in some way or other, would be a wretched society.

Man is not pure spirit, but is tied up, so far as his earthly destiny is concerned, with the realm of things. He is dependent upon the soil and the various fruits of the soil, not only for the survival of his body, but for the cultivation of his mind. Crass as the judgment may be, it is nevertheless true that the wonderful experience of listening to violin music would not be possible apart from the physical existence of horses' tails and of cats. These, and all things like them, are what we mean by property. They are not the higher life, but they make it possible.

To say that true religion is concerned with property

[1] G. A. Studdert-Kennedy, *The Wicket Gate*, Hodder and Stoughton, 1923, p. 154.

makes sense if we realize that the average man's spiritual life is so largely dependent upon possessions of some kind. The purpose of the classic injunction against stealing is not that of protecting the rich landlord from the depredations of his hungry and crowded neighbors; the purpose of the injunction is to protect the weak against the strong and to provide a solid basis which makes community possible. To steal is to deprive another of the fruits of his labor, and there are many ways of stealing, some of them temporarily lawful.

There are some, especially convinced Marxists, who speak and write as though all religion, including the Christian religion, were a conservative force, helping the rich to keep the poor people poor. In this they are following the direct lead of Lenin. But such a judgment is possible only if men close their eyes to a large part of the evidence. We, of the West, cannot speak with much confidence of conditions in the Orient, but we do know that Judaism, Christianity and Islam have all acted as forces leading to social amelioration and even social revolution. The burden of Mohamet's message was not the bolstering up of the type of Arabian society in which he was born. Judaism, as a conscious world faith, arose out of the revolutionary teachings of the great prophets whose fundamental message continues to be the real inspiration of most of those, including Marxists, who criticize an evil order in the light of a moral ideal.

Those who suppose that religion is always a method of safeguarding the rich and quieting the poor are forced to close their eyes to a great part of the record. They do not dare to look at John Woolman, for example, or to

read his *Word of Remembrance and Caution to the Rich,*
first printed in 1793. They do not dare even to open the
Bible, especially at the Gospel According to St. Luke.
On this point, as on so many others, H. G. Wood expresses the situation in a memorable sentence which we
do well to repeat as often as we can. "It is simply not
true," says Professor Wood, "to say that religion has always been and is now a purely conservative force, defending the *status quo* and keeping the poor quiet."[2]

The more we look into the matter, the more we are
impressed with the true radicalism of the Biblical tradition which we have inherited in the communal life of the
West. The developing moral code of the Bible was
greatly concerned with the protection of the common
man, the man with a small holding which he had perhaps
inherited. The evils of absentee landlordism are clearly
outlined in the work of Isaiah and other prophets. The
necessity of protecting the livings of widows, orphans
and other helpless persons is reiterated. The Book of
Deuteronomy, inspired as it is by prophetic teaching,
twice emphasizes the commandment, "Thou shalt not
remove thy neighbour's landmark."[3] Closely associated
with this is the still more enlightened observation,
"Cursed be he that perverteth the judgment of the
stranger, fatherless, and widow."[4]

We do not fully realize the degree to which the
Biblical tradition upholds the rights and dignity of the
common man until we contrast the characteristic teach-

[2] H. G. Wood, *Christianity and Civilization,* The Macmillan Co.,
1943, p. 64.
[3] Deuteronomy 19:14.
[4] Deuteronomy 27:19.

ing of the Hebrews with the characteristic teachings of their neighboring peoples in the Near East. Sometimes the contrast is so great as to be almost incredible. Thus the Tell el-Amarna tablets give contemporary evidence, all the more important in that it is unintended, of the servility toward superiors which was required and expected. A minor Syrian prince, writing to his political superior, the king of Egypt, expresses his relative situation as follows: "Ammunira, the man of Beirut, thy servant, and the dust of thy feet (hath spoken) saying: At the feet of my Lord the king, my Sun, my gods, the breath of my life, have I fallen down seven and seven times."

In contrast to this disgusting servility the Bible records the lives of a succession of poor men who are able to stand up against kings, because *both* they and the kings are *men*. Moses begins this tradition by taking the side of the oppressed in Egypt and by maintaining that Yahweh has taken their side too. Moses, the first great Biblical character who is clearly a historical and not merely a legendary character, wins his place precisely because he sides with the weak against the strong. Having been brought up in the royal Egyptian household, as the foster child of the King's daughter, Moses had every opportunity for an easy life, living luxuriously on the fruits of oppression. But, when he actually saw the oppression, he made his crucial decision and identified himself with the oppressed.[5]

We have already referred, in an earlier chapter, to the remarkable and revealing story of Naboth, with its revo-

[5] Exodus 2:11–15.

lutionary significance for human life. It is the story of how a prophet could take the side of a wronged man and denounce even the king, to his very face, because the moral law is no respecter of persons. A modern interpreter helps us, in the following sentences, to understand the uniqueness of all this:

One will search in vain in the literature of the ancient world to find anything like this. Elijah is not a priest. He has no official position of any sort. The terrible judgment he has just delivered is sedition and lese-majesty. In any other Oriental court the king's guards would have struck him down immediately without even the formality of a trial; and if his death had been delayed, it would have been only to prolong it with torture. But here, the chronicle has it, the king of Israel accepts this divine verdict of the public conscience.[6]

The same theme appears even earlier in the story of David and Bathsheba, to which we have referred in a preceding chapter. The surprising thing is not that the king, in order to have a free hand with Uriah's wife, arranged for the loyal soldier to be killed in battle. The surprising factor is that Nathan rebuked the king and that the king accepted the rebuke.

These stories might be interpreted, and have sometimes been interpreted, to mean that the true prophet must always uphold the poor against the rich. But such an interpretation is profoundly erroneous. Nathan and Elijah were not taking part in the class struggle, but

[6] Gregory Vlastos, *Christian Faith and Democracy*, Hazen Book, 1938, pp. 17, 18.

were concerned with *justice*. David was unjust to *Uriah* and the point of the Bible story is that the moral realities of the situation were not altered, in the least, by the fact that David was the king. David was denounced, not *because* he was king, but *in spite of the fact* that he was king. His kingship did not exempt him from the impartial judgment of the divine plumb line. By the same reasoning, Uriah would not have been exempt if he had been equally guilty. The fact that he was a poor man and a soldier would not have altered the situation. As the king's kingship does not exempt him from the judgment of the moral law, so the poor man's poverty does not exempt him.

It is instructive, in this regard, to note that, in the New Testament, Christ judges men by their fairness and productivity, regardless of whether they have much or little. In the parable of the talents,[7] the man who had only one talent, and used it poorly, was not exonerated on the ground that he was poor. The concept of impartial justice is a far more profound concept than is that of the class struggle.

Rich men can be predatory, but merely getting rid of the rich will not solve our human problem. Poor men can be predatory, too, and they can be equally cruel, as any violent revolution demonstrates. The elimination of wealth or even of all private property would not extricate man from his predicament, because, when private property is given up, men struggle with one another for personal status. "Those who have very little that they

[7] Matthew 25:14–30.

can call their own," says Schweitzer, "are in most danger of becoming purely egoistic."[8]

Capitalism has its inherent human dangers and evils, but the same can be said for socialism or any of the other supposed alternatives. The right ordering of property, if we take account both of human nature and of our classic moral heritage, lies not in the *elimination* of private property, but in the *distribution*, as widely as possible, of private property. The chief reason why great accumulation of wealth, such as sometimes occurs in a capitalistic society, is wrong, is not that property is an evil thing, but that property is a good thing. It is such a good thing that it ought to be part of the life of more people than is possible when a few have vast quantities.

When we note the difference which ownership makes in a community we know that the ancient doctrine, illustrated vividly by the story of Naboth, is the right theory. A community of Naboths is far better than a community of tenants can ever be. The owner, even though he be a small owner, has a real stake in the community and all its facilities, educational and recreational. He belongs. He employs human pride in the right way when he tries to keep up his homestead and give it a good appearance.

The modern movements to break up cities, to give families a small stake in the land, to make them *owners*, are movements in the main stream of the spiritual life of the West which arises in Judaism and Christianity. *Stealing is evil because ownership is good.* An important part of our moral task is to encourage ownership and to pro-

---

[8] Albert Schweitzer, *Civilization and Ethics*, p. 266.

tect against all the kinds of stealing, direct and indirect, which tend to break down the dignity of common living. It is right that honest men should own houses and automobiles, and it is right that they should be protected in the ownership of these so long as they do not harm others.

G. K. Chesterton, in his vigorous defense of this Christian ideal of property, used to compare the economic choices open to man to the marital choices open to him. When men say, as they often do, Chesterton pointed out, that we must choose between capitalism and socialism, that is like saying that a man is forced to choose between living with a harem and living as a celibate. The terrific fact is that there really *is* a third possibility, the strange and glorious possibility called monogamy. It is quite likely that this odd arrangement of one husband and one wife may be better than either the harem or the celibacy. In the same way, the supposedly dull and commonplace, but actually exciting, idea of distributed property may be better than either capitalism or socialism.

The only way in which our society can be held together is by the conviction of the people. If the tendency to pay no attention to the rights of others to keep and use what they have earned and saved should become general, there would be little that we could do about it. Certainly the law would not suffice. Our best protection is still character. The moral judgments of our neighbors save us a thousand times where the police save us once. What is frightening in this regard is that we seem to be losing ground. In many geographical areas of the West, the basis of trust once known is no longer practicable.

If we are finally forced to use lock and key for everything we value, much of what is best in life will already be gone. But it *will* be gone unless we can convince one another of a duty to our fellows which is deep and powerful because it arises from a shared relationship to a common Father.

Chapter IX

THE REQUIREMENTS OF VERACITY

Thou shalt not bear false witness against thy neighbour.

All of the short and specific commandments which those steeped in the Western heritage know and remember best are concerned ultimately with persons. In each instance an act is seen as evil, not in abstraction, but in its effect on human beings, who are precious because they are made in God's image. Killing is evil, because it is persons who suffer and die; adultery is evil, because it is a person to whom a man is disloyal when he breaks his marriage vow; theft is evil, because private property represents the blood and sweat and sometimes even the tears of other human beings. In the same way a lie is evil because it harms one's neighbor. In the other three commandments the personal basis of the evil is assumed, but in the case of false witness the ancient moral law makes the personal reference explicit. The kind of lying which is directly and specifically denounced is false witness against a neighbor. That is the kind that is really dangerous.

All these particular moral laws are merely ways of showing, in detail, what it means to uphold, in word and deed, the dignity and value of human life, including that of others as well as our own. All men seek to safeguard the dignity and value of their own lives. By the same token, our heritage asserts, we ought to seek the same for all other members of the human family, who are likewise children of a common Father. The specific moral laws are detailed applications of the true categorical imperative, which is, "Thou shalt love thy neighbor as thyself."

It is very important that the duty of truthtelling should be placed in this larger ethical setting because, superficially, it appears to become the most abstract of all the virtues. The ancient law puts truthtelling into the most important as well as the most difficult context into which it can be put. It is lies about *people* that are the most dangerous lies in the world and it is these lies which otherwise good persons are most tempted to tell.

The ninth commandment is almost universally broken and is probably more often broken than any other, with the exception of the tenth. Thousands of highly respectable persons, who would never dream of committing murder or adultery or robbery, engage in talebearing and detraction every day of their lives. It is so easy and so pleasant to sit with one's friends and discuss a third party, especially if the conversation is mildly derogatory. It is such a pleasant form of sin, since it is not one for which anyone can be sent to jail, and yet it gives a bit of excitement along with the sense of relative virtue in one's self. Just to talk of the shortcomings of another makes the conversationalist feel virtuous by contrast.

Nearly all human conversation is concerned with the deeds and character of other human beings. Most of the time we pose as amateur moralists. We say, "She ought not to have done it." "Wasn't that preposterous?" "Imagine!" "He did a good job that time." This is not to complain of our human preoccupation with one another and our deeds, but to point to an undeniable fact. It is, of course, inescapable. We are incurably interested, for good or ill, in one another, in our opinion of the acts of others and in others' opinions of our own acts. This, indeed, is the human situation. It follows necessarily from the human gift of self-consciousness, which is the root of all our higher virtues as it is likewise the root of all our most terrible vices.

Man is a creature who is persistently and painfully concerned with *reputation*. We want praise. Sometimes we want it so badly that we do almost anything to get it. That is why we cannot bear to be ridiculed. We should choose to be hated rather than despised, and despised rather than ridiculed. We build up intricate systems of honor, and when we have destroyed these by a revolution, we proceed forthwith to create new forms in which excellence is recognized. And the people who claim they do not prize such honors are probably liars.

The Japanese custom of committing suicide when there has been a loss of face is not something strange, but merely a stylized and regularized form of what all men feel in such situations. So greatly do we care about the opinions of others that we frequently take the trouble to insure their good opinion of us after we are gone, even though we are well aware that we shall not be present to enjoy this posthumous reputation. Once in a while it is possible to rise above the desire to be praised and desire rather to be truly *praiseworthy*, but that is a very high level of moral achievement. It is most understandable if it is a desire for the respect of God, the Impartial Observer, rather than the respect of finite men.

It is precisely because we care about reputation so much that we can harm one another so easily. Nearly all blackmail gets its power from the desire for good standing in the opinion of others. Thoroughgoing blackmail is, however, comparatively rare. What is common, instead, is the equally dishonest, but perhaps more cowardly effort to advance our own standing by sly insinuations concerning our competitors for place and power. Two professors of the same department, each eager to achieve a high reputation for scholarship, may be sorely tempted to say a word suggesting that the colleague has somehow missed his goal. The most successful form of this attack is faint praise. If we wish to suggest that a man's scholarship is superficial rather than deep we point out his adeptness at popularization. Equally damaging is the apparent kindness by which we mourn over the fact that it is too bad that poor Professor X's work hasn't really caught on. You can do your competitor terrible harm by pitying him in conversation with others.

Now it is against all this that the ancient moral law is directed. Its positive form, in the first place, becomes:

Thou shalt be meticulously honest in dealing with the reputations of others. There is an ancient Quaker query, which need not be limited to Quakers but can be profitably put by all men to themselves at regular intervals as a form of spiritual discipline: "Do you avoid tale bearing and detraction and are you careful concerning the reputations of others?"

The requirement that we should be careful concerning the reputation of others does not imply the abstention from criticism or even from condemnation, when these are required by faithfulness to the truth. Our ancient heritage gives no support whatever to the easy doctrine that we should always speak well either *of* other people or *to* other people. The hard words which the prophets used on many occasions, and the terrible condemnation which Christ made of the Pharisees, constitute vivid evidence that our heritage is not that of uncritical tolerance. Certainly it is not one of bootlicking.

The doctrine of uncritical tolerance has had many vocal exponents in our century and has achieved, at times, considerable popularity. Many claimed, prior to 1941, that we should not condemn the actions and policies of the Nazis, and one student, writing in the *Atlantic Monthly* as late as 1940, defended this policy of non-condemnation by asking the rhetorical question, "They think they're right, don't they?"

One of the most thorough expositions of the general doctrine of non-judgment is Dale Carnegie's *How to Win Friends and Influence People*. The point to make here is not the common one that the book is offensive to good taste, but that it represents a sharp departure from our spiritual heritage of truthtelling. "Let's realize," says Carnegie, "that criticisms are like homing pigeons. They always return home. Let's realize that the person we are going to correct and condemn will probably justify himself, and condemn us in return."[1] Of course. But what of it? The question is not whether we may incidentally have trouble, but whether the right prevails. Such a position as that stated above never reaches the ethical plane at all, but stays on the level of *prudence*, which is a totally different matter. In order that the doctrine of non-condemnation under all circumstances shall be better understood, Mr. Carnegie goes on with the following specific proposition:

Instead of condemning people, let's try to understand them. Let's try to figure out why they do what they do. That's a lot more profitable and intriguing than criticism; and it breeds sympathy, tolerance, and kindness. "To know all is to forgive all."[2]

Of course we must criticize. All men, including ourselves, do terrible evil and the truth must be told. The danger is that we shall adopt an easier standard for our own conduct than we adopt for the conduct of others. The solution of the problem lies, not in the abstention from all criticism, but in the achievement of genuine objectivity, which is what the golden rule requires. Our aim must be to deal with *any* human action, be it ours or another's, with that kind of impartiality which plays no favorites either in praise or blame. It means to have *one*

[1] Pocket Book Edition, p. 30.
[2] *Ibid.*, p. 36.

context, which includes both ourselves and our neighbors. The problem would be solved if we could combine human tenderness with the objectivity of judgment which the higher levels of scientific discovery so often illustrate. The central moral paradox is that the ethical endeavor, which aims solely at the welfare of persons, is best achieved when we refuse to be respecters of persons. *The ultimate claims of personality are advanced by a rigorous impersonality.*

Though truthtelling is chiefly concerned with the relations between persons, it is so good a thing that it must be extended to all the relations of life. Actually we do find it already very highly prized in some wholly impersonal relations. The most striking instance of this is the way in which many men and women who work in scientific laboratories are extremely careful of the exact truth, both in the conduct of experiments and in the announcement of their results. This is one of the most instructive as well as encouraging aspects of modern experience.

That the success of science rests on ethical foundations is clear to all who bother to consider the question. Apart from this high ideal of personal honesty most of our advanced technological work would not be possible. The work of the laboratory is such that men could cheat in their announced results if they should choose to do so. Often there is no qualified observer to deny what is said. Another experiment can, of course, be performed and it may give different results, but there is frequently no way of proving that the man who conducted the first experiment lied about *it*. In short, here is an area where trustworthiness is required and where falsehood would be disastrous to the entire enterprise. We are more conscious than we were of the moral basis of science in view of the recent experiment, observed by the whole world, in which the work of science was limited by extraneous factors, such as that of race. There is a good deal of evidence that German science declined when its ancient moral basis was so largely undermined. It was not the Nazi scientists, devoted to Aryan physics, who first learned to release the atomic power of uranium. What exquisite justice there is in the fact that the basic mathematical work for this undertaking was done by a Jewish woman, driven away by the Aryanizing of science.

Fortunately for us and for the world, the meticulous regard for the truth is still the dominant tendency among us in regard to *things*, though it may not be of people. It is a curious paradox, but nevertheless true, that we are more careful in what we say about atoms than we are in what we say about men.

The deepest question is that of the general view of the world and its meaning which makes truthtelling so important. Why should a man be so finicky about a formula or a measurement? There is nothing sacred about figures and nothing sacred about things. Only persons are really sacred. Why is truth so august and compelling? Would it be august and compelling if this were a merely materialistic or mechanical world, utterly devoid of the kind of meaning which purpose alone can give? The late Archbishop Temple has rendered a service to philosophy and to common life by his insistence on this point, especially in the following words:

Willingly to believe what is suspected to be false is felt to be not only a degradation of the credulous believer's personality, but an offence against the order of reality. This feeling is quite unreasonable if the order of reality is a brute fact and nothing else; it is only justifiable if the order of reality is the expression of a personal mind, for the sense of moral obligation towards Truth is of that quality which is only appropriate in connexion with personal claims.[3]

Since reverence for persons is the ultimate basis of all morality, in a world which is fundamentally personal, because it is a world of meaning and purpose, it is easy to see that truthtelling is of paramount importance. Truthtelling is of paramount importance, not because of loyalty to the things *about which* we tell, but because of the persons *to whom* we tell. Falsification is wrong, because it means taking advantage of the person who trusts us. The only possible excuse for falsification of any kind is that of loyalty to persons, in that they might be harmed if the falsification did not occur.

The most practical form which the categorical imperative takes is this: *Thou shalt be trustworthy*. This is the positive commandment which is obviously more significant for human welfare than any negative commandment in the world. And this is the practical point on which the greatest possible emphasis must now be placed as we look to the reconstruction of a world so largely in ruins. All the elaborate plans which we make

[3] William Temple, *Nature, Man and God*, The Macmillan Company, 1934, p. 250.

about the control of the atomic bomb are bound to fail of their purpose *unless those who agree to the controls are personally trustworthy.*

This analysis helps us to realize why it is that we tend to put so much emphasis, and rightly so, on the keeping of promises. *A good man is a man who keeps his promises.* If he promises to pay, he will finally do so if he possibly can, even though it kills him. The world is helped more by that kind of faithfulness than it is by the continued life of one individual man. A wise man is careful in *making* promises, but a good man is meticulous in *keeping* them.

Here, then, is the perfect illustration of the theme of this book. The theme of this book is that the reconstruction of our world is not primarily a problem in engineering and not primarily a problem in politics, important as both are, but that the underlying task is to recover the sense of a moral order. Unless this is the foundation of the temple of man, they labor in vain that build it. This may seem, at first, to be pious and conventional talk. But when we come to the problem of trustworthiness, almost any man can see the validity of the argument. This is the Achilles' heel of a merely secular civilization.

Chapter X

THE COUNTERPOISE OF GREED

~~~~~~~~

Thou shalt not covet anything that is thy neighbor's.

The first article of an ethical creed has the advantage of priority, but the last article has the advantage of finality. It is reasonable that the problem of greed should engage our attention at the end of the classic series, because greed, in its many forms, is the last enemy of both noble and ignoble minds. So great is the power of greed in men's lives that we shall never overcome it wholly, so long as we are finite men. We cannot eradicate it, but we can learn to recognize it in its various disguises and find some ways of living in which the power it represents is balanced by an equal and opposite power.

The universality and pervasiveness of greed we cannot doubt. Popularly it is envisaged as greed for money or for material things, but this is only one of the many forms which covetousness takes. This the ancient law suggests by naming several possible objects of cupidity. There are many who do not covet money, but who nevertheless covet power or prestige or status. The greed for praise is often far stronger than greed for wealth and, even when wealth is greatly desired, it is usually desired not for its own sake but because of the relative power over other men which it makes possible. It is inherent in the human situation that we are deeply and universally concerned over the problem of *station*. We want to stand well in the eyes of our fellows, and one of the easiest ways of securing their flattering service is to have ascendancy over them. Even our communistic Utopias fail because it is so easy to eradicate the love of wealth and yet keep the love of prestige.

It is part of the sophistication of the Biblical morality that all this is clearly recognized. That, it would seem, is the reason why the tenth commandment of the Decalogue is reserved for the conclusion of the series. The last sin is the most difficult sin. Just as there is a positive moral law which underlies all the specific moral laws concerning the sacredness of life, of marriage, of ownership and of veracity, so there is a temptation which underlies all other temptations, bringing all the particular aspects of the good life into constant jeopardy. The pervasive fact of human greed constantly endangers life itself, because men will sacrifice even the lives of other men to achieve their own greedy ends; it constantly endangers the sanctity of marriage, in that unbridled lust is merely one of the forms which the love of power takes, often involving much more than mere physical desire; it constantly endangers the dignity of ownership because we covet the possessions which other men have, and therefore find subtle ways of justifying ourselves when we take them; it constantly endangers the structure of mutual trust, because greed will make us distort the truth in order to degrade our competitor or to elevate ourselves in relation to him. The sophistication of the classic formulation lies in the fact that it goes beyond overt actions to the source of actions, and that it puts the final emphasis on the motive rather than the deed.

The recognition of the power, the universality and the pervasiveness of greed is very important for us both practically and theoretically, especially in the construction of economic and political systems. This is really the rock on which all authoritarian systems of dictatorship break. An authoritarian system, like that of the late Benito Mussolini, gains much of its initial success from its realistic estimate of human nature. It is maintained, in such a system, that men are weak and self-regarding. Because of this, they cannot be trusted, but must be controlled, even for their own good. They are so stupid that you cannot trust them to vote. You cannot, the argument proceeds, have a stable order unless the populace is regimented, both physically and psychologically. Therefore you must have both thought-control and the strategy of terror, of which the concentration camp is the chief instrument. The purpose of the concentration camp, in this system, is not primarily the punishment of the innocent men who happen to be imprisoned in it, but in the fear which their stories puts into the hearts of the populace. The conviction is that most men are such cowards that this ruthless power, once recognized, will never be seriously challenged, for each individual man is afraid to run the risks involved.

Much of this is very shrewd. The dictator's estimate of human nature is not wholly accurate, as the resistance movement finally proved, but much of it is undoubtedly justified by experience. Yet, logically, there is a fatal flaw in the system. For some unaccountable reason it fails to recognize the necessary implication that the leaders will themselves exhibit the venality which they expect in the rest of the human race. The doctrine of original sin is no respecter of persons! If all men are potentially corrupt, as the authoritarian systems hold, this *must* include the leader, since the leader is also a man. The fascist system, therefore, stands self-condemned because it really proclaims that the leader cannot be trusted, *yet it has provided no checks and balances upon him, in case he becomes untrustworthy.*

The vast contemporary importance of this is that it shows the fundamental reason why democracy is not merely a passing political fashion, but actually the best way in which human life can be ordered. The most profound argument for democracy is not the assertion that men are essentially rational, trustworthy and good, for they are not. They are full of prejudices and they may be swept away by fierce and irrational hatreds. The most profound argument for democracy is the realization, fundamentally Biblical in origin, that the love of power is so pervasive and so inordinate that democracy, which means a system of mutual checks, *even upon the ruler*, is the only alternative to injustice and oppression.

Democracy is the best way of life, not because all men are virtuous and reasonable, but because all men are greedy. The government exists primarily to curb the wanton exercise of power, either in any faction or in any individual man. *Democracy is necessitated by the fact that all men are sinners; it is made possible by the fact that we know it.*

It is instructive to note, not only the theoretical, but the actual historical connection between the Biblical view of man and our emerging democracy. Few thinkers are as important in this connection as the great Richard Hooker, whose famous book at the end of the sixteenth century *seemed* to concern only ecclesiastical polity, but really concerned the foundations of civil polity as well. "Laws politic," he wrote, "ordained for external order and regiment among men, are never framed as they should be, unless presuming the will of man to be inwardly obstinate, rebellious, and averse from all obedience unto the sacred laws of his nature."[1] The reason we must institute an impartial system of rewards and punishments, says Hooker, is "because the greatest part of mankind prefer their own private good before all things, even that good which is sensual before whatsoever is most divine."[2]

Important as a theoretical defense of the necessity of democracy may be, the practical problem of how we can make democracy work in the modern world is even more important. In spite of the fact that democracy is the best way to organize human life, it can break down and it *does* break down unless the proper spirit can be maintained. Wherever the amount of corruption and bribery passes a certain decisive point, democracy no longer

[1] *Laws*, I, x, 1.
[2] *Laws*, I, x, 5.

works, no matter how good the constitution may be on paper. Democratic government, with its checks on all, is more likely than is any other form of government to *avoid* this excessive corruption, but even *it* is not foolproof or, what is more to the point, knave-proof.

The consequence of this is that our democracy, which is the standard order of the West, must be continually supported by what amounts to moral and spiritual revivals. Since the machinery of government will not suffice, no matter how ingenious it may be, there must always be the cultivation of those forces in society which do actually make men more trustworthy. Mere government, without the cultivation of good will, will eventually face secession, while mere good will, without government, will be unable to deal with the occasional fits of self-assertion to which the human race is liable.

The problem of greed, then, has two answers, neither one of which we dare omit. The first answer is to recognize the existence of greed in all men and to arrange legal ways of curbing the worst abuses to which it leads. *This is the external answer.* The second answer is to bring to bear on human life the power which most mitigates greed, that of genuine conversion. *This is the internal answer.*

Pervasive as greed may be, it is nevertheless a fact that men can have such a sense of the love of God that much of their natural cupidity is purged away. When this occurs, we are still men, with all the temptations to which creatures in our finite state are heir, but we can become new men. The power of greed is so great that it cannot be handled, in the end, except by a still greater power, the redemptive power of Almighty God. The ultimate verification of our religion consists of the changed lives to which it can point and for which it is responsible in such impressive numbers through the centuries. It is our shame that the number of truly changed lives has been so few; it is our hope that the number of truly changed lives has been so many.

If we could find in our day even a few men who had the gift to lead other men to the revolutionary experience of the transforming love of God, as when St. Francis led thousands to give up oppressive luxury, or John Wesley encouraged common men to become honest citizens, we should be wise to give them every facility for their work. Our money would be well invested. A dozen such men would do more for world reconstruction than would a thousand policemen or a whole division of troops of occupation. For though the power of the police or the occupying army may *curb* greed and the desire for revenge the power of faith *attacks* these at their source.

We have sought, in this book, to change all the classic prohibitions into positive commands. We have sought, not arbitrary rules, but underlying principles of moral action. But the last of the ten commandments is the most difficult of all to put into positive form. It is easy to see that the positive counterpart of the injunction against murder is the principle of the sacredness of life and that the positive counterpart of the injunction against adultery is loyalty to a chosen mate, but what is the positive counterpart of the warning against greed?

As we try to meet this question seriously we are driven

to an embarrassingly simple answer. The counterpart is none other than that which the New Testament calls *agape* and which we really ought not to translate, because any translation is a distortion of what is infinitely precious. The counterpoise of greed is *agape,* which cannot be defined except by using an entire chapter in the New Testament.[3] *Agape* envieth not, vaunteth not itself, seeketh not its own. It is not something from our natural world, but it is something which, by God's grace, has come *into* our natural world to save us before it is too late. This, then, is the conclusion of the matter. *Love completes the law.*

In this great matter we must summon the courage to be truly simple, because the analysis of our situation, though difficult, leads to a simple answer. One of the most reliable thinkers of our time has had the courage to put the matter so straightforwardly that we can do no better than to use his words.

What the world today needs is Christian individuals with real depth and power. Such individuals will become the centers of this creative and redeeming fellowship wherever they are. They will become the nuclei of growing and multiplying cells. We need men today whose will to live has been freed from the will to power, to success, to superiority, to social recognition, to possession and to pretense; and has found its peace and power in the will to love, the will to fellowship, the will to self-giving service, the will to do God's will and to be His children.[4]

It is often said in our time that what the world needs

[3] I Corinthians 13.
[4] Nels Ferré, *Return to Christianity*, Harper & Brothers, 1943, p. 36.

is religion. This may be true, but the deeper question is: what kind of religion? There are many kinds of religion. But there is *one* kind of religion which has proved itself able to make new men and to inspire and support new societies. It is the religion which knows only one absolute and that is the kind of love which makes men *care* so deeply for their neighbors, whoever they are, that they feel their neighbors' sufferings as their own. There are many stones in the foundation on which we must build, but this is the cornerstone.